The Literature of Theology

The Literature of Theology: A Guide for Students and Pastors

Revised and Updated

David R. Stewart

Westminster John Knox Press
LOUISVILLE • LONDON

The first edition of *The Literature of Theology: A Guide for Students and Pastors* was written by John A. Bollier and published in 1979 by The Westminster Press.

Cover design by Mark Abrams

Revised edition
Published by Westminster John Knox Press
Louisville, Kentucky

This book is printed on acid-free paper that meets the American National Standards Institute Z39.48 standard. ∞

PRINTED IN THE UNITED STATES OF AMERICA

03 04 05 06 07 08 09 10 11 12 — 10 9 8 7 6 5 4 3 2 1

Library of Congress Cataloging-in-Publication Data

Stewart, David R.
    The literature of theology : a guide for students and pastors /
    David R. Stewart.—Rev. ed.
      p. cm.
    Rev. ed. of: The literature of theology / John A. Bollier. 1st ed. 1979.
    Includes bibliographical references and index.
    ISBN 0-664-22342-7
    1. Theology—Bibliography.   I. Bollier, John A., 1927–Literature
    of theology. II. Title.

Z7751.B67 2003
[BR118]
016.23—dc21   2002193394

For Elizabeth,
whose
generosity, forbearance, and encouragement
have helped make this book possible

Table of Contents

Foreword

One day in a casual conversation in the library, I mentioned to David Stewart how helpful John Bollier's book, *The Literature of Theology*, had been to me when I was trying to find my way in the field, and that it could probably use updating. Without blinking an eye, he said, "I'm doing it." As pleased as I was at the news then, I am even more pleased now to be able to commend the finished product.

As a theology teacher, I have found that library tours and presentations on the bibliographic resources needed for learning how to do research are not as effective with students, especially beginning students, as one might hope. Most students stop and reflect on where to begin research only when faced with a specific assignment. How to begin going about research and more important, learning how to go deeper after making a beginning acquaintance with a field, can be daunting to beginners because they are trying both to learn the field and the research methods for interpreting it simultaneously. This revised edition of a most helpful tool will eliminate much trepidation and anxiety.

In reading the revised edition, I had to go no further for help than the introduction, where I picked up new Web addresses, for example; but Websites come and go. The more important contribution of the book is the help it will give in orienting students to the types of resources available in the various fields of study subsumed under the term *theology*. The book is not, however, only of use to beginning theology students, but also to advanced students brave enough to venture outside the narrow confines that increasingly border "the disciplines."

The revised edition happily includes the study of spirituality pioneered by outstanding scholars and attentive publishing houses over the past thirty years. In conjunction with the growth of medieval studies, and increasing attention to Eastern Orthodox Christianity, it has changed the shape of the field. By including these, *The Literature of Theology* (revised edition) will itself contribute to providing a more balanced approach to theological study.

Ellen T. Charry

Introduction

"The man who does not read good books has no advantage over the man who can't read them." So runs a quote attributed to Mark Twain, the only difficulty being that he may never have said it.* A minor conundrum such as this one—finding a ready-for-use gem of wisdom, but not *really* knowing, or being able to verify, its source—is one good way of illustrating the purpose of this book.

I heard a sermon that began with the disclaimer, "I'm not going to ask you to do a lot of thinking . . . it is, after all, Sunday morning." There is no denying that setting the cognitive bar this low has a certain folksy appeal—"people have enough to think about without *my* taxing their intelligences for another thirty minutes"—but it has some limitations as a ministry model. When John Bollier (who wrote *The Literature of Theology* in 1979) and I met in Princeton in the fall of 1998 to discuss a revision, he reflected that, while he was a seminary student in the 1950s, the ministry was still considered one of the "learned professions," recognized by the community as having its own defined body of knowledge. At that time a pastor was expected to be one of the best-informed members of the community. Unless I am missing something, the world is becoming a more, not less, complicated

---

*http://www.twainquotes.com/Book.html

place in which to live, think, work, and worship. And it seems to me a good, wise, and reasonable thing for people to expect that in our study, teaching, and preaching we ought to be supporting them within this complexity by every means available to us. Among other things, this requires of us hard, intelligent work, involving the very best tools and resources at our disposal: the "literature of theology."

While *The Literature of Theology* can do little about how much industry students, teachers, and pastors bring to their work, it does take direct aim at identifying for them the best tools once they *get* to work. Such an endeavor requires some explanation: to begin with, how does this revision differ from the first edition? As I have looked at the original work, and spoken with colleagues here and there about a revision, the high regard for both the author and the book have always been evident, even more than two decades after its appearance. Because this work was done carefully and well, it has remained much more useful than many comparable books from the late 1970s. Yet this durability in itself presents a quandary, because not only the literature itself but the media and process for study have witnessed comprehensive changes. The range and contours of what is published, the way that people study theology, and the way that libraries support those endeavors—all have argued for a different structure than what was used in the original edition.

The most obvious changes have been associated with technology: a generation ago, it hardly needed to be mentioned that many crucial aspects of theological research could be carried out only within the walls of a library. A bibliographic search, for example, required a library visit. The fact that the catalogs of all the major libraries can now be searched online from the home or office affects directly what needs to be emphasized and what needs to be included in this revision.

This raises immediately the question of why this revision is principally a guide to print, rather than to electronic, sources. Hasn't the rise of online catalogs been followed by an eclipsing of print by electronic media? At a conference reception in Boston in June 1997, John Bollier and I had our first conversations about the prospect of collaborating on a revision, and one of his concerns was for the need to incorporate electronic resources. This made perfect sense, and I admit that as I got involved in this project I assumed that in identifying "the best" in theological research resources, a significant proportion of those would be in electronic format. Yet, as I have surveyed what is available, the signs of such a shift occurring on a broad scale are few and far between. This may change, but it is simply not the case at the present time.

My work with electronic resources in the library of Princeton Seminary gives me an awareness and appreciation of them and of the features they offer that print cannot (primarily the capacities for keyword searching and for access to resources beyond the walls of the library). In our library we offer a broad range of net-worked CD-ROM sources, and have spent a lot of time configuring access to Web-based databases. Yet these are expensive, and no library can offer such resources except within strict licensing arrangements. We are fortunate to have electronic versions of *The Anchor Bible, Word Biblical Commentary,* and *BibleWorks 5,* for example, as well as Web-based resources such as *Books in Print, Acta Sanctorum, Patrologia Latina, ATLA Religion Database, Dissertation Abstracts,* and so on. But no one who studies here expects that what the library pays for and offers within a campus network will be available to them at no cost once they leave, any more than they assume they will have access to a book and journal collection such as this library offers when they complete their studies and move to a parish afterward.

So it would be a welcome side effect if this work were to put to rest, at least for the time being, the persistent myth that someday, everything will be available to everyone, everywhere, free-of-charge. Dr. Johnson's adage that "no one but a blockhead ever wrote, except for money," applies no less to electronic publishing than to print, in spite of popular folklore. People who work hard at research and writing, and the publishers who bring the fruit of their labors to market, still require and deserve fair compensation.

I have found the discipline of identifying the best sources, and of actually handling and using them in compiling annotations of more than five hundred works for this book, to be something of a surprise and a rediscovery. Again and again I felt a sense of respect and admiration at the energy and intellect being invested into a greater variety of reference books than ever.

All this is to say that this revision is still primarily a guide to resources in print, for the simple and indisputable reason that it is here that the best resources are found. Where a comparable or parallel resource is available in some electronic form, of course that is noted. An appendix maps out a selection of public-domain Websites in a structure parallel to the arrangement of print resources annotated in the book.

Beyond this, the major structural change in this work is the comparatively brief space I have allotted to what John Bollier referred to as "General Works." I have included instead a chapter of what might be considered "Basic Resources," which almost everyone in this field could at least consider acquiring (a kind of "desert island" collection). This has permitted more space for citations of works within the more descriptive subject areas (Bible, History, etc.). Also, because it is my observation that the importance of these two areas has begun to be acknowledged during the past generation (and is likely to increase), I have added brief chapters on "Christian Spirituality" and "Christianity and Literature."

Readers will observe some unevenness in both the length of citations and in the number of citations assigned to various subject areas. The former can be explained by the fact that "some excellent books are more excellent than others," and it somehow would not seem right for me to apologize for occasionally letting my enthusiasm show. (I learned that this can be a good thing while reviewing a very fine related work, William M. Johnston's *Recent Reference Works in Religion: A Guide for Students, Scholars, Researchers, Buyers, and Readers*, revised ed. [Chicago and London: Fitzroy-Dearborn, 1998].)

Over the imbalance of available published resources for given fields I have no control at all: it is a simple fact that there are far more titles available, for example, on world religions, or on matters relating to the Catholic Church, than there are on practical theology or on Pentecostalism. Perhaps the recognition of such deficits will prod an occasional reader of this book to remedy the imbalance by writing a reference book herself. (Johnston's book mentioned above included an appendix with the delightful title of "Reference Books That Cry Out to Be Written.")

The original notion was for the revision of *The Literature of Theology* to be a joint effort between the author of the original, Rev. John A. Bollier, and myself. We first discussed this when I was still working in Vancouver, and the idea of working together became more practical once I moved east in 1998. We met once in Princeton (November 1998) and once at Union Theological Seminary in New York (March 1999). Shortly afterward, John quite reasonably decided that he had postponed his retirement for too long already, and politely withdrew from the project. I admit to having had some occasional misgivings about going it alone— John had done this before, after all, and I had not—but I can at least make an honest claim to have worked hard to produce a revision that lives up to the standard set by the original.

There have been a few more surprises: first, while I write (as John did) as someone who came to theological librarianship after first serving in parish ministry, I have found it helpful to reflect on the changing role of the library. This is because (thanks largely to the Web and keyword-based search engines) I am writing for people who are accustomed to depend somewhat less, or at least in different ways, on librarians for information retrieval than was the case in 1979. Many who will find the present book most helpful are people who have access to their own range of electronic resources for communication, for discussion, for online news and current events, and for basic quick-research purposes. For those constantly engaged in their own processes of research and information retrieval, this book will help provide access to critical resources that are simply not within their reach via the World Wide Web.

The second unexpected factor has been the amount of continuity possible between the original work and this revision. In the early stages of the work, I would have anticipated that perhaps as much as 50 percent of the works cited in 1979 might still be considered the best sources available, and thus merit inclusion in the second edition. While it has meant far more work for me, it should be good news for users of this book that the "renewal" of the literature has been so substantial that on almost every subject something newer and better has become available.

It was important to me to keep the dimensions of the revision the same as the original (about 200 pages, citing and annotating about 500 works), so I have stayed within the limits of monographic literature, published in English. In some cases, I have included citations of works that are no longer in print: one of the curious blessings of the World Wide Web is that it has extended the lives of many a print volume, rescuing them from oblivion by making it easy to obtain copies cheaply even once they go out of print. In all such cases I have checked online book vendors to verify availability. (Good sources include www.powells.com, www.allibris.com, and www.abebooks.com.) An extended list of Web resources is included in Appendix 3, pages 135–42.

Working with hundreds and hundreds of books, and writing annotations for them, is mostly solitary work (often carried out in the early morning before the library opened), and this has made the help, conversation, and encouragement of others all the more welcome. To begin with, I honor John Bollier, who kindly welcomed me as a prospective collaborator when he hardly knew me, graciously entrusted the revision to me when he felt unable to continue, and who in his work and manner taught me much that I needed to learn about theological librarianship. Brantley Gasaway, now a Ph.D. student at UNC–Chapel Hill, worked with great diligence in the spring of 2001 on surveying the literature, and his fine work and collaboration were a constant pleasure. Interest and encouragement from colleagues at the Robert E. Speer Library at Princeton Seminary have been much appreciated. The caliber of its reference collection owes a lot to the wisdom and industry of Don Vorp, collection development librarian for many years. Kate Skrebutenas, reference librarian, knows this collection better than anyone, and has been invaluable as an insightful friend and colleague since the first day I arrived for work here in September 1998. Don McKim, editor at Westminster John Knox (himself the author of several works cited in this book), has been encouraging and patient, never once using the word *deadline* even though I have missed several of them.

Finally, I thank my wife Elizabeth, for being a better student than I have ever been, for respecting the importance of this project without being directly involved in it, and for providing support and encouragement throughout the process.

Chapter 1

Basic Resources

N o one who reads this book will own personal copies of all the 500 or so items that it cites and annotates; only a fortunate few will live close enough to a theological library large enough to contain them. Thus it is a helpful thing to ask, If one can only buy so many books, or if one is starting to build a personal collection (for home, study, or office), what are some recommended titles? The emphasis in this brief selection is on quality and breadth: works that cover the most ground, while at the same time being the most enjoyable and rewarding to use, and that provide at least suggestions for further research.

Selections are arranged under the following categories:

General Reference
Bible Resources
The Church in History
Christian Thought
World Christianity and World Religions
Christian Spirituality
Christianity and Literature

General Reference

1. Barrett, David B., et al., eds. *World Christian Encyclopedia: A Comparative Survey of Churches and Religions in the Modern World.* 2nd ed., 2 vols. New York: Oxford University Press, 2001.
   The definitive fact book of Christianity worldwide, in its more than 20,000 denominations. Sections on cultures, persons, a dictionary, and of course statistics in profusion. Unique and all but indispensable. Volume 1 describes the world by country, volume 2 by segments. Profiles in massive tabular and statistical detail show the status of Christianity (as well as other religions) in the modern world. Details on specific countries, religious groups, ethnic groups, on 7,000 major cities, etc., are treated in two volumes totaling about 1,600 pages. Appendices include a detailed directory of organizations and an extensive bibliography.

2. Carroll, Bret E. *The Routledge Historical Atlas of Religion in America.* New York and London: Routledge, 2000.
   A vivid and easy-to-use visual guide to the subject, beginning with indigenous cultures and extending to the end of the 20th century, with the growth of other world religions and new religions in America. Provides a clear and accessible blend of maps, charts, and text. There is also a chronology and list for further reading.

3. Cross, F. L., and E. A. Livingstone, eds. *The Oxford Dictionary of the Christian Church.* 3rd ed. London and New York: Oxford University Press, 1997.
   The definitive and indispensable work of its type in English, this volume serves principally (though by no means solely) as a source for historical material, and is especially noteworthy for the number of subjects covered and the range of contributors involved. Most articles include bibliographies.

4. Dowley, Tim, ed. *Atlas of the Bible and Christianity.* Grand Rapids: Baker, 1997.
   A historical atlas, beginning with the Old Testament period and extending to the modern church. The last section of this work offers a helpful visualization of mission activity and church growth since the Reformation era. Includes index and gazetteer.

5. Mead, Frank S., and Samuel S. Hill. *Handbook of Denominations in the United States.* 11th ed. Nashville: Abingdon, 2001.
   The most recent edition of the standard field guide to religious groups (Christian and otherwise) in America. Includes tables, bibliographies, and index.

Bible Resources

6. Douglas, J. D., ed. *New Bible Dictionary*. 2nd ed. Downers Grove, Ill.: InterVarsity Press, 1996.

   Compresses an extraordinary amount of entries and detail into one volume. This work has been revised extensively since its appearance in 1962, and an attempt has been made to incorporate new cultural and archaeological material. All except the very shortest entries include some bibliographies. There are some maps and tables, and a general index at the conclusion.

7. Mays, James L., ed. *The HarperCollins Bible Commentary*. San Francisco: HarperSanFrancisco, 2000.

   Includes seven introductory essays on the Bible in its historical and cultural settings, along with helpful introductions to each section of the Scriptures. Commentaries on individual books (including the Apocrypha) include their own introductions and basic bibliographies.

8. Metzger, Bruce Manning, and Michael D. Coogan, eds. *The Oxford Guide to Ideas and Issues of the Bible*. New York: Oxford University Press, 2001.

   This volume updates the earlier *Oxford Companion to the Bible*. Unlike a Bible dictionary, this work treats not only subjects within the Bible, but those associated with the Bible and with its understanding through history. It is a good source for providing an introduction to a Bible theme or subject. The articles tend to be brief, and a fine bibliography is included at the end.

9. Rogerson, John. *The Oxford Illustrated History of the Bible*. Oxford: Oxford University Press, 2001.

   This volume covers the topic under three broad headings: the Making of the Bible (a. Historical Background, b. Text and Translation), the Study and Use of the Bible, and Contemporary Interpretation. Eighteen extended essays by distinguished contributors are included. The illustrations (in color and black-and-white) are extensive, and complement the text extremely well.

The Church in History

10. Bromiley, Geoffrey, ed. and trans. *The Encyclopedia of Christianity*. 5 vols. projected. Grand Rapids: Eerdmans; Leiden: Brill, 1999–.

    Based on the 3rd ed. of the German *Evangelisches Kirchenlexikon*, and thus the vast majority of the articles are written from a non–North American perspective. The historical coverage comes close to comprehensiveness, and more than most reference works this one reflects the globalization of Christianity. Its articles are lengthy, and the bibliographies that accompany them are excellent.

11. Reid, Daniel G., ed. *Dictionary of Christianity in America*. Downers Grove, Ill.: InterVarsity Press, 1990.
    A fine and substantial (1,300+ pp.) collection of articles on everything related to the panorama of Christian life and culture in America. There is an attractive balance between entries on persons, ideas, movements, institutions, etc., and this work succeeds in covering a vast and diverse subject in one volume. Short bibliographies accompany entries.

Christian Thought

12. Alexander, Desmond, ed. *New Dictionary of Biblical Theology*. Leicester and Downers Grove, Ill.: InterVarsity Press, 2001.
    This three-part work (Introduction, Biblical Corpora and Books, Biblical Themes) is devoted mostly to longer, topical essays, and to discussion of theological issues raised by genres of biblical literature. Articles include bibliographies, and a general index is included.

13. Hart, Trevor A., ed. *The Dictionary of Historical Theology*. Carlisle, Cumbria, UK; Waynesboro, Ga.: Paternoster Press; Grand Rapids: Eerdmans, 2000.
    About 300 entries in a volume of just less than 600 pages means that articles are more lengthy than in most works of this kind (and that the editor has been selective in deciding what to include). This selectiveness is more than compensated for by the excellent bibliographies that accompany individual articles, and by the detailed index. Generally this work provides a fine starting point for readers to begin research in the field.

14. Hastings, Adrian, Alistair Mason, and Hugh Pyper, eds. *The Oxford Companion to Christian Thought*. Oxford: Oxford University Press, 2000.
    The purpose of this expansive volume is to "provide a lively introduction . . . to a living tradition of thought central to the world and, in modern times, to global civilization" (p. ix). In spite of the range of topics covered, most of the articles are several pages in length, and conclude with helpful bibliographies. This is the kind of reference work that can be profitably used either with a specific topic in mind or simply browsed at leisure.

15. McGrath, Alister E., ed. *The Blackwell Encyclopedia of Modern Christian Thought*. Cambridge, Mass.: Blackwell, 1993.

A collection of major essays on central themes, including pieces on philosophical movements. Though it is not produced on quite the same scale as the *Oxford Companion* (#14), it stands as a very strong source for introductory research. (Example: the Robert Detweiler essay on "Postmodernism" is a terrific overview of an often poorly defined subject.) Both a glossary and an index are included.

16. Musser, Donald W., and Joseph L. Price, eds. *A New Handbook of Christian Theologians.* Nashville: Abingdon, 1996.

This volume limits its attention to theologians of recent times, and is a good source in instances when the reader needs a concise overview of a given theologian's life, context, and work. Bibliographies with each article are brief but useful. Generally this work offers fewer subjects than a larger dictionary, but at greater length.

World Christianity and World Religions

17. Hinnells, John, ed. *Who's Who of World Religions.* New York: Simon and Schuster, 1992.

This work offers concise biographical entries on hundreds of key figures of many different religions, set out alphabetically. The 450+ pages of entries are complemented by an outstanding general bibliography, maps, and index.

18. *Macmillan Compendium of World Religions.* New York: Macmillan, 1997.

An excellent one-volume dictionary (just short of 1,300 pages). Entries include an overview of the subject, bibliographic surveys, and notes on the history of study for that subject. Because it does all these things well, and because of its length, this dictionary serves as a fine entry point for one who wants to begin with basic information as well as receive direction on where to look for a larger view. The index is about 70 pages in length.

Christian Spirituality

19. Magill, Frank N., and Ian P. McGreal, eds. *Christian Spirituality: The Essential Guide to the Most Influential Spiritual Writings of the Christian Tradition.* New York: Harper & Row, 1988.

An outstanding descriptive guide to the literature of Christian spirituality, covering writers from Clement of Alexandria to Gustavo Gutíerrez. Each of the 125 selections is given an introduction and accompanied by a recommended reading list. Example: Walter Hilton's "The Ladder of Perfection": introductory material provides dates and an overview of his life and work. Key themes are noted. A four-page overview of "The Ladder of Perfection" is followed by a short recommended reading list.

20. Van de Weyer, Robert, ed. *The HarperCollins Book of Prayer: A Treasury of Prayer Through the Ages.* San Francisco: HarperSanFrancisco, 1993.
     Arranging prayers in historical sequence by author, this volume presents, in the author's words, "not so much an anthology of prayers, as a collection of people praying" (p. 9). Each entry includes a brief biographical sketch. A general bibliography and an index of topics round out the work.

21. Wakefield, Gordon S., ed. *The Westminster Dictionary of Christian Spirituality.* Philadelphia: Westminster, 1986.
     This dictionary comprises about 400 pages of succinct articles, including individual bibliographies. It attempts to provide a balanced coverage for Orthodox, Roman Catholic, Protestant, and other traditions. The articles are concise but useful in providing an introduction or starting point for study on a given topic.

Christianity and Literature

22. McGrath, Alister, ed. *Christian Literature: An Anthology.* Oxford, UK, and Malden, Mass.: Blackwell, 2001.
     This compendium of almost 800 pages arranges 90 selections into five periods (patristic through modern). Each is "framed" with introductory remarks, and, where possible, sources for further reading are included. Any single work that encompasses selections from Cyril of Jerusalem to Bede to William Langland to George Herbert to Graham Greene is bound to be selective, but this work succeeds admirably both at illustrating the incredible richness of the Christian literary tradition and at placing this feast within reach of students at all levels. Includes a bibliography and index.

Chapter 2

Books about the Bible

The volume and range of resources available in support of Bible study has never been greater than it is at present. Because there are so many fine items available, and because their titles and functions seem at times to overrun one another, to put them to proper use it is helpful to be able to categorize them according to their intended purpose.

The following selection of more than 70 items has been divided as follows:

Bibliographic Resources
Archaeology and Atlases
Background and People
History and Interpretation
Language and Literature
Dictionaries, Companions, and Handbooks
Biblical Theology

It is good to be reminded that these are *reference* works. Almost always they serve as the best possible point of entry for getting information on a given subject, and surprisingly often they cover the subject so well that further searching is not required.

What these books do best is provide an insightful and concise summary of how a given subject has been studied and understood, as well as suggested sources for further research. There are distinct critical advantages to beginning with a source of this type, rather than foraging through the library (or bookstore) shelves in search of what we hope will be useful books: time saved, more information in a briefer format, currency of information, etc.

Bibliographic Resources

23. Bauer, David R. *Biblical Resources for Ministry: A Bibliography of Works in Biblical Studies.* 2nd ed. Nappanee, Ind.: Evangel, 1998.
    A thorough list of citations (without annotations) of resources for the study of the Bible. Includes sections on the entire Bible, each of the Testaments, and an appendix on Bible software programs. The main contribution of this work is to provide a nonevaluative list of what is available.

24. ———, ed. *Bibliographies for Biblical Research: Old Testament Series.* 32 vols. Lewiston, N.Y.: Mellen Biblical Press, 1997–.
    This series charts out the literature of recent Old Testament scholarship. As with the corresponding New Testament series, subjects are assigned to scholars who are conversant with the topic and with what is being published in the field. Citations are grouped by chapter and verse, subject, and so on. Bible commentaries are listed separately.

25. Brown, Raymond E. *An Introduction to the New Testament.* New York: Doubleday, 1997.
    The bibliographic resources cited (including the extensive footnotes) in this introduction are remarkable. At the conclusion of each section, the author sets out a vast array of sources, many of which have been cited in the course of his introduction. There are appendices on "The Historical Jesus" and "Jewish and Christian Writings Pertinent to the New Testament," as well as author-title and subject indexes.

26. Carson, D. A. *New Testament Commentary Survey.* 5th ed. Grand Rapids: Baker, 2001.
    Critically evaluates introductions, theologies, and so on, as well as various types of commentaries. The author scrutinizes not only individual works, but the overall caliber and evenness of series such as the Anchor Bible, Hermeneia, etc. This is one instance in which the reader especially wants the author's frank opinions, and in this Carson does not disappoint.

27. Chamberlin, William J. *Catalogue of English Bible Translations.* New York, Westport, Conn., and London: Greenwood, 1991.

The purpose of this work is to provide a comprehensive list of Bibles (or parts of the Bible) in English since the earliest appearance of translations. Volumes are indexed chronologically, and are grouped by sections of the Bible. There is a bibliography and an index of translators, editors, and translations.

28. Fitzmyer, Joseph A. *An Introductory Bibliography for the Study of Scripture.* Rome: Editrice Pontificio Instituto Biblico, 1990. *Luke*

 A distinguished New Testament scholar provides a wide-ranging list of sources for the benefit of beginning students. Citations are annotated, and arranged according to format of material and by subject. Describes more than 700 titles, with journal review citations provided for each entry. An excellent bibliographic resource.

29. Harrington, Daniel J. *The New Testament: A Bibliography.* Wilmington, Del.: M. Glazier, 1985.

 The best thing about this bibliography is its extensiveness, yet it is weakened by the lack of annotations and is now in need of updating. The list follows first the structure of the New Testament, and then includes topics in New Testament theology and other issues. An author index is included.

30. Longman, Tremper. *Old Testament Commentary Survey.* Grand Rapids: Baker, 1995.

An annotated review not only of commentaries but of Old Testament reference works generally (histories, introductions, atlases, etc.). The list of works evaluated is extensive and varied, and the author's evaluative comments are insightful and frank. Two appendices address affordability and map out an "ideal" reference library.

31. Mills, Watson E., ed. *Bibliographies for Biblical Research: New Testament Series.* 21 vols. Lewiston, N.Y.: Mellen Biblical Press, 1993–.

The idea behind this series is to commission a distinguished scholar in a given field or book of the Bible to compile a list of sources. Though a series like this needs frequent updating, it provides a thorough inventory of New Testament scholarship. Citations are grouped in various ways: chapter and verse, subject, etc. Commentaries are listed separately.

32. Mills, Watson E. *Critical Tools for the Study of the New Testament.* Lewiston, N.Y.: Mellen Biblical Press, 1995.

A thorough, carefully annotated inventory of research sources of almost every kind, including periodicals, book reviews, grammars, lexicons, software programs, theology libraries, and many others. The risk of writing a book like this is how quickly it becomes incomplete (especially with regard to software), but this book represents a good summary of works up to the date of its publication.

Archaeology and Atlases

33. Aharoni, Yohanan, and Michael Avi-Yonah. *The Macmillan Bible Atlas.* 3rd ed. New York: Macmillian, 1993.
   This volume is more text-oriented than some other Bible atlases. Maps are arranged by historical period, from the Canaanite period up to the Second Jewish Revolt against the Romans. A very helpful approach, and a fine resource for teaching purposes. Maps are clearly indexed. A chronological table and index are included.

34. Braybrooke, Marcus. *The Collegeville Atlas of the Bible.* Collegeville, Minn.: Liturgical Press, 1998.
   The color plates and illustrations in this work are beautiful, and the chronological arrangement of material (Old and New Testaments by period) makes it easy to use. There are not many maps, however, so this work serves more accurately as an illustrated companion to the Bible. There is a brief index.

35. Brisco, Thomas V. *Holman Bible Atlas: A Complete Guide to the Expansive Geography of Biblical History.* Nashville: Broadman & Holman, 1998.
   A chronological visualization of the biblical world. This atlas demonstrates an ideal balance between text and image, illustrating the entire biblical period up to the early church just prior to Constantine. There is a glossary, a fine bibliography, and an index of peoples and places.

36. Cleave, Richard. *The Holy Land Satellite Atlas.* Vol. 1: *Terrain Recognition.* Nicosia, Cyprus: Rohr Productions, 1996.
   A completely new approach, using images captured via satellite photography as well as conventional maps, charts, and landscape photography. Rather than using the conventional chronological approach, this work provides collections of images of specific locations (Plain of Sharon, Negev, Wadi Arabah, etc.). The contribution these vivid images offer to the richness of topographic detail and to the sense of geographical scale is impressive. The accompanying text has been provided by leading scholars.

37. Coogan, Michael D., ed. *The Oxford History of the Biblical World.* New York: Oxford University Press, 1998.
   This work employs twelve lengthy scholarly essays (each by a different scholar) on different phases of Bible history (pre-Israel through Roman

Empire) to cover the subject. Well presented, with numerous black-and-white illustrations, and a section of color plates. Each essay includes its own bibliography. There is a chronology, a general bibliography, and an index.

38. Dowley, Tim, ed. *Atlas of the Bible and Christianity.* Grand Rapids: Baker, 1997.
    See #4.

39. Mazar, Amihay. *Archaeology of the Land of the Bible, 10,000–586 B.C.E.* New York: Doubleday, 1990.
    A chronological approach to the subject. Beginning with an outline of the nature of archaeological work in the Holy Land, Mazar describes how this science has been applied to successive periods of Old Testament history. There are abundant illustrations throughout, and two indexes.

40. Meyers, Eric M., ed. *The Oxford Encyclopedia of Archaeology in the Ancient Near East.* 5 vols. New York and Oxford: Oxford University Press, 1997.
    An expansive treatment of the subject, including lengthy articles, numerous charts, maps, illustrations, and chronologies. The bibliographies that follow individual articles are excellent. There are several appendices to the final volume, including maps, chronologies, and a synoptic outline of contents.

41. Negev, Avraham, ed. *The Archaeological Encyclopedia of the Holy Land.* Revised and updated edition. New York: Continuum, 2001.
    An A–Z approach to the places, topics, and issues of biblical archaeology. The entries tend to be concise, and this volume will be especially useful where a brief topical sketch rather than an extended scholarly discussion is wanted. Contains maps, charts, illustrations, chronological tables, and glossary.

42. Pritchard, James B., ed. *The Harper Atlas of the Bible.* New York: Harper & Row, 1987.
    This reference work brings together large-format maps, plates, and illustrations with outstanding scholarly historical overviews and a wealth of supporting material, such as a time line, an index of persons, and a gazetteer. The atlas follows a comprehensive historical sequence, extending from prehistory to the Christian Era.

43. Rasmussen, Carl G. *Zondervan NIV Atlas of the Bible.* Grand Rapids: Zondervan, 1989.
    An illustrated, region-by-region survey of the geography of the Bible, followed by a historical survey. This atlas is more text-oriented than

some other titles, and in this respect functions somewhat more as a textbook than a visual sourcebook. There are extensive endnotes, a lengthy bibliography, and an index.

44. Stern, Ephraim. *Archaeology of the Land of the Bible*. New York: Doubleday, 2001.
    Covers the Assyrian and Babylonian periods (732–332 B.C.) in an illustrated, encyclopedic manner. A scholarly approach.

Backgrounds and People

45. Evans, Craig E., and Stanley E. Porter, eds. *Dictionary of New Testament Background*. Downers Grove, Ill.: InterVarsity Press, 2000.
    "Attempts to situate the New Testament and early Christianity in its literary, historical, social and religious context" (p. ix), incorporating approximately 300 articles. The emphasis is on articulating ideas and themes crucial to an understanding of the setting of the New Testament. Articles are substantial in length, and include extensive bibliographies. Scripture, subject, and title indexes are included.

46. Finegan, Jack. *Handbook of Biblical Chronology: Principles of Time Reckoning in the Ancient World and Problems of Chronology in the Bible*. Peabody, Mass.: Hendrickson, 1998.
    This two-part study outlines first the way chronology was reckoned in the ancient world, and second, specific problems of chronology within the biblical texts.

47. Gardner, Paul, ed. *The Complete Who's Who in the Bible*. London: Marshall Pickering, 1995.
    Entries arranged A–Z on persons appearing in the Bible. The entries range in length from a few lines to several pages. There are no bibliographies, but those are to be expected not from a ready-reference source such as this one but from a proper Bible dictionary.

48. Gruber, Mayer I. *Women in the Biblical World: A Study Guide*. Vol. 1: *Women in the World of Hebrew Scripture*. Lanham, Md.: Scarecrow, 1995.
    A comprehensive and scholarly bibliographical guide to the subject, covering women in the ancient Near East. Subheadings by type of source (dissertations, books, articles) and by specific regions, periods, and peoples provide a manageable approach to an impressive body of literature.

49. Hayes, John. *Who Was Who in the Bible*. Nashville: Nelson, 1999.

Without any introduction, index, or bibliography this work presents an A–Z range of entries on people of the Bible. The articles provide pronunciation aids and English translations for biblical names. Line drawings are interspersed throughout.

50. Metzger, Bruce Manning, and Michael D. Coogan, eds. *The Oxford Guide to Ideas and Issues of the Bible.* New York: Oxford University Press, 2001. See #8.

51. ———, eds. *The Oxford Guide to People and Places of the Bible.* Oxford: Oxford University Press, 2001.
    In restricting its subject to people and places, a volume like this one essentially extracts entries that would normally be presented in a more general Bible dictionary. This serves as a useful subset for readers whose interests regularly follow the narrower range of topics included. There are maps and an index.

52. Meyers, Carol, ed. *Women in Scripture.* Boston: Houghton Mifflin, 2000.
    In its depth and scope this volume functions as a specialized dictionary. In addition to the entries on women in the Bible, there are supporting general essays on aspects of scholarship. These are well done, but their specific relation to the topic of the book is not always obvious. Entries are grouped under three headings: Named Women, Unnamed Women, and Female Deities and Personifications. There is a list of ancient sources as well as a bibliography at the conclusion.

53. Porter, J. R. *The Illustrated Guide to the Bible.* London and New York: Oxford University Press, 1995.
    Few works combine so well as this one the complementary nature of image and text. This work presents a developmental survey of the making of the Scriptures, from the beginning of Genesis to the end of Revelation. A separate "Reference File" at the conclusion contains a book-by-book summary, glossary, index, and resources for further reading.

History and Interpretation

54. Ackroyd, Peter R., et al., eds. *Cambridge History of the Bible.* 3 vols. Cambridge: Cambridge University Press, 1978–1980.
    Volume 1 extends from the Beginnings to Jerome; vol. 2, the West from the Fathers to the Reformation; vol. 3, the West from the Reformation to the Present Day (i.e., date of this work's publication). This massive subject is treated through a collection of essays by individual scholars

(example: C. K. Barrett on "The Interpretation of the Old Testament in the New," in vol. 1). Bibliographies accompany each of these essays, and a general bibliography is added at the end, along with indexes.

55. Adam, A. K. M., ed. *Handbook of Postmodern Biblical Interpretation.* St. Louis: Chalice, 2000.
    Forty essays provide an overview of how biblical interpretation has been reshaped by postmodernist thought. Articles are devoted about equally to topics ("Deconstruction," "Intertextuality") and persons ("Bakhtin," "Lyotard"). A superb general bibliography and an index round out the volume.

56. Coggins, R. J., and J. L. Houlden, eds. *A Dictionary of Biblical Interpretation.* London: SCM; Philadelphia: Trinity Press International, 1990.
    This work provides an A–Z approach to the major topics, trends, and issues in biblical interpretation. Articles are followed by brief but thoughtful bibliographies. Subject and Scripture indexes conclude the work.

57. Elwell, Walter A., and J. D. Weaver, eds. *Bible Interpreters of the Twentieth Century: A Selection of Evangelical Voices.* Grand Rapids: Baker, 1999.
    Brief sketches of leading conservative Protestant interpreters (e.g., Bruce Metzger, R. K. Harrison), which provide the reader with a sense of the work they did and the milieu in which they worked.

58. Gugliotto, Lee J. *Handbook for Bible Study: A Guide to Understanding, Teaching, and Preaching the Word of God.* Hagerstown, Md.: Review and Herald, 1995.
    This well-crafted work brings together in about 400 pages a variety of resources, including surveys on exegetical methodology (6 chapters) and an extensive section on language study. The latter covers the subject from the basics of grammar through literary types to evaluation of various English translations, to consideration of how the biblical canon was shaped. Appendices include a bibliography, a directory of software resources, a section devoted to the Letter of Jude, and a selection of reproducible worksheets.

59. Hayes, John H., ed. *Dictionary of Biblical Interpretation.* 2 vols. Nashville: Abingdon, 1999.
    A comprehensive resource serving as a "guide to the lengthy and complex history of biblical interpretation" (p. xlix). The work includes three types of entries: major articles on the history of interpretation, shorter pieces on individual interpreters, and articles reviewing and

discussing influential methods and movements in interpretation. The bibliographies accompanying the articles are extensive.

60. McKim, Donald K., ed. *Historical Handbook of Major Biblical Interpreters.* Downers Grove, Ill.: InterVarsity Press, 1998.

This work comprehends a vast subject by dividing it into six broad historical periods, extending from the early church through to 20th-century North America. Within these divisions, substantial essays are included on figures from Jerome to Bullinger to Griesbach to Gunkel to Albright. The individual bibliographies for these essays are outstanding. Indexes of persons, subjects, and essays and articles are included.

61. Rogerson, John. *The Oxford Illustrated History of the Bible.* Oxford: Oxford University Press, 2001.

See #9.

62. Sæbø, Magne, ed. *Hebrew Bible, Old Testament: The History of Its Interpretation.* 3 vols. Göttingen: Vandenhoeck & Ruprecht, 1996–.

This work provides an outstanding examination of the history of scholarly study of the Old Testament from earliest times. This scholarly work approaches branches of this subject in painstaking detail (example: chapter 10: "The Reception of the Origenist Tradition in Latin Exegesis"), and the footnotes and bibliographies are correspondingly extensive. Includes name, subject, and Scripture indexes.

Language and Literature

63. Balz, Horst, and Gerhard Schneider, eds. *Exegetical Dictionary of the New Testament.* 3 vols. Grand Rapids: Eerdmans, 1990–1993.

This work is a guide to the forms, meaning, and uses of every word in the 3rd edition of the *Nestle-Aland Novum Testamentum Graece.* The bibliographies included in the individual articles are extensive. It should be noted that since this work was translated from an earlier work in German, the bulk of the citations are of non-English works.

64. Baumgartner, Walter, Ludwig Koehler, and Johann Jakob Stamm. *The Hebrew and Aramaic Lexicon of the Old Testament.* 5 vols. Leiden: E. J. Brill, 1994. (Also available in CD-ROM edition.)

This English translation of an earlier German original from the 1950s is well on its way to replacing the older Brown, Driver, and Briggs (BDB) lexicon as the standard resource of its kind. The layout is similar to BDB, with each entry including roots, variants and cognates, biblical examples, and citations for further study. The first volume includes an extended bibliography of works, mostly in German and English, and the rest of the Hebrew portion of the dictionary fills out the succeeding three volumes. The fifth, supplementary volume (with its own bibliography) is devoted to Aramaic.

65. Bergant, Dianne. *The Collegeville Concise Glossary of Biblical Terms.* Collegeville, Minn.: Liturgical Press, 1994.
    Rather than using the usual A–Z approach, this work considers major terms in order of their biblical appearance. Hence it begins with "Myth" and "Legend" in the Genesis creation stories, and concludes with the terms "Serpent," "Satan," "Devil" in the book of Revelation. Includes a basic index.

66. Botterweck, G. Johannes, et al., eds. *Theological Dictionary of the Old Testament.* Grand Rapids: Eerdmans, 1977–.
    English translation of *Theologisches Wörterbuch zum Alten Testament.* The primary function of this standard work is to provide complete lexical resources (etymology, syntax, etc.) for the vocabulary of the Old Testament. The emphasis on *Theological* in the title indicates this work's added interest in an integrative development of ideas, traditions, etc., within the entire Old Testament canon. Longer entries typically include a section on a term's basic meaning, its history, its theological development throughout the canon, etc. Bibliographies are included for most articles; there are extensive footnotes.

67. Cairns, Alan. *Dictionary of Theological Terms.* 2nd ed. Belfast: Ambassador, 1998; Greenville, S.C.: Emerald House Group, 1998.
    In spite of the title, the entries in this work are of greater length than one would expect from a dictionary. (Example: more than a full page on "Infralapsarianism," pages 192–94; 21 pages on "Textual Criticism of the New Testament," pages 373–94.) Important Latin as well as English terms are defined (*"Opera ad intra,"* etc.). There is no bibliography or index.

68. Danker, Frederick William, ed. *A Greek-English Lexicon of the New Testament and Other Early Christian Literature.* 3rd ed. Chicago: University of Chicago Press, 2000.
    This is the most recent revision of the standard lexicon for students and pastors. Intended for those at least somewhat familiar with Greek. The range and depth of textual resources considered is dazzling, and yet one of the strengths of this work is that it can be of use at a variety of levels: it can be referred to simply as a dictionary (providing plenty of scriptural cross-references) or for much more complex textual matters.

Extensive bibliographical references are interwoven throughout.

69. Friberg, Timothy, Barbara Friberg, and Neva F. Miller. *Analytical Lexicon of the Greek New Testament.* Grand Rapids: Baker, 2000.
Like its antecedents, this work offers less detail than other lexicons (#68, etc.) but brings together all the forms of a given Greek word in one entry. This approach is particularly useful to Greek students whose grasp of forms is still developing.

70. Jenni, Ernst, and Claus Westermann, eds. *Theological Lexicon of the Old Testament.* Trans. Mark E. Biddle. 3 vols. Peabody, Mass.: Hendrickson, 1997.
English version of *Theologisches Handwörterbuch zum Alten Testament.* Somewhat less daunting than #66 but slightly older (its German original was completed in 1976). Helpful statistical tables and thorough indexes conclude the third volume.

71. Kittel, Gerhard, and Gerhard Friedrich, eds. *Theological Dictionary of the New Testament.* Trans. Geoffrey W. Bromiley. 10 vols. Grand Rapids: Eerdmans, 1985.
This standard resource combines elements of a lexicon with those of an encyclopedia, as its interest is not only in etymology and meaning but in more integrative concerns such as tradition and theology. Entries are arranged by root word, rather than in strict alphabetical sequence. A longer entry typically includes a section on a term's broader Hellenistic usage, Old Testament antecedents and parallels, usage in Rabbinic Judaism, all prior to considering the term in its New Testament setting. Bibliographies are included for most articles; there are also compendious footnotes.

72. Moulton, James Hope, and G. Milligan. *The Vocabulary of the Greek Testament.* Peabody, Mass.: Hendrickson, 1997.
This is a reprint of the 1930 edition, which attempted to bring together data from the papyri regarding New Testament words. A work of this vintage misses out on the lexical discoveries and advances of more recent scholarship, yet its thoroughness and relative ease of use have kept it on the shelves of many students and pastors. Entries are keyed numerically to *Strong's Concordance.*

73. Ryken, Leland, James C. Wilhoit, and Tremper Longman, eds. *Dictionary of Biblical Imagery.* Downers Grove, Ill.: InterVarsity Press, 1998.
This work takes the measure of an aspect of understanding the Bible that is rarely given much consideration by Bible dictionaries and encyclopedias: the variety and complexity of biblical language, includ-

ing imagery, symbolism, metaphors, etc. There are entries on "humor," "gestures," "wind," etc. Articles include bibliographies, and there are Scripture and subject indexes.

74. VanGemeren, Willem A., ed. *New International Dictionary of Old Testament Theology and Exegesis.* 5 vols. Grand Rapids: Zondervan, 1997.

    Newer than Botterweck (#66), a substantial early part of this work's five volumes is devoted to theology and exegesis. There are four distinct parts: a guide to Old Testament theology and exegesis, about 3,000 lexical and topical entries, an extended cross-reference system, and an entire volume of detailed indexes. Most of its resources do not require a knowledge of Hebrew.

75. Verbrugge, Verlyn, ed. *The NIV Theological Dictionary of New Testament Words.* Grand Rapids: Zondervan, 2000.

    An abridgment and thorough revision of the earlier *New International Dictionary of the New Testament* (which itself was based on an earlier German work). Major changes in the present volume include a greater emphasis on access for the English reader, assigning each Greek work a numerical key, etc. Many of the extensive bibliographies from the earlier, larger work have been abridged. This one-volume version achieves a satisfactory compromise between depth of research and accessibility and convenience.

76. Würthwein, Ernst. *The Text of the Old Testament.* Rev. ed. Grand Rapids: Eerdmans, 1995.

    A standard text outlining in detail the textual traditions that underlie our current Old Testament. Discusses (and illustrates) in detail the origins, distinctives, and value of how these textual sources form the basis of our present translations. The indexes are extensive.

Dictionaries, Companions, Handbooks

77. Achtemeier, Paul J., ed. *The HarperCollins Bible Dictionary.* San Francisco: HarperSanFrancisco, 1996.

    This volume offers some of the best contemporary biblical scholarship in an accessible one-volume format. There are limited black-and-white illustrations and maps (and a short section of color plates in the middle). Many articles include short bibliographies.

78. Bowker, John Westerdale. *The Complete Bible Handbook.* New York: DK Pub., 1998.

    A volume as richly illustrated as this one inevitably functions differently from one that is more text-oriented: with a work like this the reader is looking at, as well as reading about, the world of the Bible. (DK Pub. is renowned for the caliber of its illustrations.) There are three sections: Old Testament, New Testament, and Reference (incorporating people and places in the Bible). A glossary and bibliography are included.

79. Brown, Raymond E., et al., eds. *The New Jerome Bible Handbook*. Collegeville, Minn.: Liturgical Press, 1992.
   Based on, and complementing, the *New Jerome Biblical Commentary* (#107). A book-by-book introduction to the basic structure and content of the Bible (including the apocryphal literature). There is also a section of general articles on inspiration, canonicity, archaeology, Paul, etc. The format of this book indicates that it is intended for the student at the introductory level.

80. Browning, W. R. F. *A Dictionary of the Bible*. Oxford and New York: Oxford University Press, 1996.
   This book offers a text-only alternative, comprising generally brief entries on themes, persons, and places of the Bible. Intended to provide quick-reference information rather than the basis for further study (there are no bibliographies except, very briefly, at the end. Tables of weights and measures, time line, bibliography, and maps conclude the work).

81. Butler, Trent C., ed. *Holman Bible Dictionary*. Nashville: Holman Bible Pub., 1991.
   A vividly illustrated and creatively designed dictionary, including both short and major articles, NASA-generated maps, color illustrations, etc.

82. Douglas, J. D., ed. *New Bible Dictionary*. 2nd ed. Downers Grove, Ill.: InterVarsity Press, 1996.
   See #6.

83. ———, ed. *The New International Bible Dictionary*. Grand Rapids: Zondervan, 1987.
   This volume falls somewhere in the middle of the available Bible dictionaries between brevity and exhaustiveness. Updates and abridges extensively the earlier *Zondervan Pictorial Bible Dictionary*. Most of the longer articles include bibliographies. Illustrations and maps are in black-and-white. There is an extensive Scripture index.

84. Freedman, David Noel, ed. *Anchor Bible Dictionary*. 6 vols. New York: Doubleday, 1992.
   The heavyweight of recent Bible dictionaries, in terms of scale, num-

ber of contributors, etc. Differs from most other dictionaries not only in the number of subjects treated but in the depth of coverage and the range of supporting resources (maps, charts, bibliographies, though fewer pictures than most comparable works). The vastness of this work is not indicative of its being exclusively intended for advanced scholars. This work commends itself for those particular instances where greater detail is required.

85.   ———, ed. *Eerdmans Dictionary of the Bible*. Grand Rapids: Eerdmans, 2000. This work offers approximately 5,000 articles in the space of about 1,500 pages, from more than 500 contributors. Includes black-and-white illustrations and a small selection of maps. The articles vary in length from several lines to several pages, with the longer entries including bibliographies. For its sheer breadth of coverage, this volume offers everything that can be expected of a one-volume treatment.

86.   Hastings, James A., ed. *A Dictionary of the Bible: Dealing with Its Language, Literature, and Contents, Including the Biblical Theology*. 5 vols. Reprint Peabody, Mass.: Hendrickson, 1988. This work has remained in print for over a century, a fact that attests to its thoroughness and its appeal to readers with an appreciation for the history of biblical scholarship. Still useful, though of course dated.

87.   Kee, Howard Clark, et al., eds. *The Cambridge Companion to the Bible*. Cambridge; New York: Cambridge University Press, 1997. A well-indexed and well-researched source on the Bible within history, cultures, and various communities of faith. Essays are lengthy and rich. There are excellent charts and extensive bibliographies.

88.   Manser, Martin H., ed. *The Hodder Dictionary of Bible Themes*. London: Hodder and Stoughton, 1996. Published in the U.S. as *The Zondervan Dictionary of Bible Themes*. Grand Rapids: Zondervan, 1999. This volume serves as a combination of handbook and concordance, providing a thorough thematic index to the Bible. A variety of indexes provide the reader with several points of access: themes are listed alphabetically, keyed to numeric entries, and integrated with a Scripture index. This volume's unique arrangement takes some getting used to, but offers a useful integrative approach to the Bible's major themes.

89.   Mills, Watson E., ed. *Mercer Dictionary of the Bible*. Macon, Ga.: Mercer University Press, 1990. The collaborative work of more than 200 Baptist-affiliated scholars, treating topics in the usual alphabetical arrangement. Some black-and-

white maps and illustrations, and a fine separate collection of color plates.

90. Selman, Martin J., and Martin H. Manser, eds. *The Macmillan Dictionary of the Bible.* London: Macmillan, 1998.
    The comprehensiveness and detail of longer dictionaries are not always called for. This volume of about 200 pages provides a quick-reference alternative, with very brief entries, maps, and charts.

91. Youngblood, Ronald F., ed. *Nelson's New Illustrated Bible Dictionary.* Nashville: Nelson, 1995.
    This work brings together text, color plates, and maps to provide a good introduction and overview to the Bible and its world. Since the entries are usually short, and they do not include bibliographic sources, it serves best as a resource for basic research and for quick and specific information, rather than as a starting point for more detailed study.

92. ———, ed. *Nelson's New Christian Dictionary.* Nashville: Nelson, 2001.
    This extended quick-reference source supports ready reference or fact checking. In addition to the articles in the main section of the book, there are 22 appendices, providing essays on diverse subjects. The function of a work like this is slightly different from a standard Bible dictionary in giving greater than usual prominence to most important books and authors in Christian literature.

Biblical Theology

93. Alexander, Desmond, ed. *New Dictionary of Biblical Theology.* Leicester, UK, and Downers Grove, Ill.: InterVarsity Press, 2001.
    See #12.

94. Elwell, Walter A., ed. *Baker Theological Dictionary of the Bible.* Grand Rapids: Baker, 1990.
    This work is designed for the reader who does not have a working familiarity with the biblical languages, and endeavors to make available coverage of the principal theological themes and topics within the Bible. Less emphasis is devoted to scholarly debate than to outlining the Bible's own development of theological ideas. The longer entries have concise bibliographies. A Scripture index is included.

95. Green, Joel B., and Scot McKnight, eds. *Dictionary of Jesus and the Gospels.* Downers Grove, Ill.: InterVarsity Press, 1992.
    The idea behind this volume is to bring together in the space of just less than 1,000 pages as much as possible of recent scholarship on this

vast subject: everything from introductory discussions for students to comprehensive surveys and up-to-date reviews. Articles are extensively cross-referenced. Bibliographies accompany articles, and multiple indexes are included.

96. Hawthorne, Gerald F., and Ralph P. Martin, eds. *Dictionary of Paul and His Letters*. Downers Grove, Ill.: InterVarsity Press, 1993.
    This volume endeavors to collect and bring together in one place the best of newer scholarship on Paul and the Pauline letters. It functions, then, as a specialized and concentrated kind of Bible dictionary, with all the entries integrated by their relation to the thought, life, and teaching of Paul and his circle. With each of the articles comes a fine bibliography. Indexes of Scripture, subject, and articles are included.

97. Martin, Ralph P., and Peter H. Davids, eds. *Dictionary of the Later New Testament & Its Developments*. Downers Grove, Ill.: InterVarsity Press, 1997.
    A companion volume to ##95 and 96 (volumes on Jesus and the Gospels and Paul and his letters). The intention is to bring together the best in recent scholarship to shed light on the study of *Hebrews, Jude, 1 Peter,* etc. Good bibliographies and indexes, and all the more valuable because this part of the New Testament writings is often neglected. The bibliographies accompanying the articles are superb; Scripture, subject, and article indexes are comprehensive.

98. McDonald, Lee Martin, and Stanley E. Porter, *Early Christianity and Its Sacred Literature*. Peabody, Mass.: Hendrickson, 2000.
    Somewhat in the style of the earlier *New Testament Foundations* (R. P. Martin), this volume sets out an intelligent and well-organized framework for scholarly study of the New Testament. Some black-and-white illustrations. Excellent bibliographies, tables, indexes.

99. Stuhlmueller, Carroll, ed. *The Collegeville Pastoral Dictionary of Biblical Theology*. Collegeville, Minn.: Liturgical Press, 1996.
    This valuable Roman Catholic work begins with a collection of major scholarly essays on subjects relating to biblical interpretation. This is followed by about 1,000 pages of entries on topics A–Z. Cross-references between articles are very useful. It is highly unusual for a work of this scope not to provide bibliographic resources.

Chapter 3

Bible Commentaries

C ommentaries at times seem to be one category of reference work where there is no such thing as "enough." Every year, publishers' catalogs introduce not only new commentaries, but (seemingly) new entire *series* of commentaries.

While one appreciates the amount of intellect, study, and industry that this represents, to many students the overall effect is overwhelming. It can have the unintended effect of leaving the mere mortals among us—whose grasp of the languages may not be complete, or whose exegetical skills are not at an expert level—with a sense of inadequacy. It is not unusual for students to buy more than they will ever need, or to buy "bargains" based on heft or "shelf presence"; yet over time such commentary purchases become nothing more than excess baggage. (There is some merit in saving money by consulting "classic" commentaries like John Calvin or Matthew Henry, in public domain and in online editions, for example, http://www.ccel.org, rather than purchasing them.)

A good piece of practical advice I received while studying theology was to purchase one good set of commentaries for each of the testaments, and then to identify what is reputed to be the best commentary for each individual book of Scripture, and over time purchase that.

The commentaries listed here are intentionally limited to one-volume approaches and to series covering either the entire Bible or either the Old or New Testament. The commentary surveys by Longman (#101) and Carson (#100) are included to offer assistance to those who wish to look for independent volumes.

Selections are arranged under the following categories:

Bibliographic Sources
Guides to the Bible
Commentaries in One Volume
Commentary Series

Bibliographic Sources

100. Carson, D. A. *New Testament Commentary Survey.* 5th ed. Grand Rapids: Baker, 2001.
     See #26.

101. Longman, Tremper. *Old Testament Commentary Survey.* Grand Rapids: Baker, 1995.
     See #30.

Guides to the Bible

102. Alter, Robert, and Frank Kermode, eds. *The Literary Guide to the Bible.* Cambridge: Harvard University Press, 1987.
     Approaches the biblical books as literary genres, and from that standpoint seeks to provide the student with a better understanding of how the Bible speaks. Each book of the Bible is assigned to an individual literary/biblical scholar, and each of these treatments includes a list of suggested further readings. General essays on the nature of biblical literature conclude the volume.

103. Longman, Tremper, and Leland Ryken, eds. *A Complete Literary Guide to the Bible.* Grand Rapids: Zondervan, 1993.
     A very useful work, which includes introductory chapters on understanding the Bible as literature, sections on the literature of the Old and New Testaments, and finally reflections on the literary influence of the Bible. Each chapter has its own bibliography, and there is a general index.

Commentaries in One Volume

104. Barton, John, and John Muddiman, eds. *The Oxford Biblical Commentary.* Oxford: Oxford University Press, 2000.

Three introductory essays are followed by individual book-by-book commentaries, including the apocalyphal literature. There are maps at the end, and the bibliographic resources are extensive. Bibliographies conclude each book commentary, and the "Bibliographical Guide to Biblical Studies" (pp. 1330–45) is outstanding.

105. Bergant, Dianne, and Robert J. Karris, eds. *The Collegeville Bible Commentary: Based on the New American Bible with Revised New Testament.* Collegeville, Minn.: Liturgical Press, 1989.

An anthology of separately commissioned booklets by 34 Catholic scholars on various sections and individual books of the Bible. At least two features common to most single-volume commentaries are lacking here (likely explained by the way this work was compiled): (1) An ensemble of integrative introductory essays usually provides a helpful framework for the individual book commentaries. This volume has only one of these. (2) Bibliographic resources are largely overlooked. Even in the case of a commentary strictly for laypeople, these are unfortunate omissions. Includes color maps.

106. Boring, M. Eugene, Klaus Berger, and Carson Colpe, eds. *Hellenistic Commentary to the New Testament.* Nashville: Abingdon, 1995.

A translation and adaptation of the German *Religionsgeschichtes Textbuch zum Neuen Testament.* Gathers related excerpts of Greek literature and presents them in the context of related New Testament texts for illustration and comparison.

107. Brown, Raymond E., et al., eds. *The New Jerome Biblical Commentary.* Englewood Cliffs, N.J.: Prentice-Hall, 1990.

An update of the earlier (1968) one-volume Catholic commentary on the Scriptures. There are general, topical articles, as well as commentaries on the individual books. Each section begins with its own brief bibliography, and there is a general bibliography and index at the conclusion.

108. Carson, D. A., et al., eds. *New Bible Commentary: 21st Century Edition.* Downers Grove, Ill.: InterVarsity Press, 1994.

A comprehensive revision of the 1953 original based on the NIV. Includes introductory essays to the major sections of the Bible, as well as black-and-white maps and tables.

109. Farmer, William R., ed. *The International Bible Commentary: A Catholic and Ecumenical Commentary for the Twenty-First Century.* Collegeville, Minn.: Liturgical Press, 1998.

A distinguished and thorough approach, incorporating some fine introductory essays (on history of interpretation, liturgical use, textual transmission, pastoral concerns) with commentaries on the individual books. These commentaries provide introduction to major themes, helpful outlines, historical and textual background, and section-by-section (rather than word-by-word) exposition. Bibliographies accompany both the introductory essays and the individual commentaries. Maps and indexes are included.

110. Friedman, Richard Elliot. *Commentary on the Torah: With a New English Translation.* San Francisco: HarperSanFrancisco, 2001.
     A commentary in the Jewish tradition on the books of Moses. The author includes the Hebrew text and his own English translation with an extensive commentary. His intention is to provide commentary in the classic tradition, but with the benefit of recent advances in archaeology, history, literary structure, and social sciences.

111. Keener, Craig S. *The IVP Bible Background Commentary: New Testament.* Downers Grove, Ill.: InterVarsity Press, 1993.
     This work endeavors to bring to light for general readers the cultural and historical background critical to understanding the Bible. In this respect it brings together what would more commonly be found in a Bible companion within the structure of a commentary. This background is offered in introductions to each book of the New Testament (e.g., "Genre," "Authorship") as well as in the chapter-by-chapter commentaries. In essence, this work fills in cultural distinctives that would have been obvious to the contemporary observer but are typically obscure to the Bible reader of the twenty-first century. A very useful innovation in Bible commentaries. Includes maps, charts, and basic bibliography (following the introduction).

112. Mays, James L., ed. *The HarperCollins Bible Commentary.* San Francisco: HarperSanFrancisco, 2000.
     See #7.

113. McGrath, Alister E. *The NIV Bible Companion: A Basic Commentary on the Old and New Testaments.* Grand Rapids: Zondervan, 1997.
     A more concise mode of interaction and summary than what is offered in most single-volume commentaries, this work is especially suited to introductory or quick-reference purposes.

114. Mills, Watson E., ed. *Mercer Commentary on the Bible.* Macon, Ga.: Mercer University Press, 1995.
     Produced by the National Association of Baptist Scholars of Religion, this work includes general articles and commentaries on apocryphal or

deuterocanonical books as well as those of the Bible. Each commentary has brief information on authorship, setting, interpretation, an outline, etc. The commentaries themselves are concise and offer a general, noncritical overview. Bibliographies are limited but useful.

115. Newsom, Carol A., and Sharon H. Ringe, eds. *The Women's Bible Commentary.* Louisville: Westminster John Knox, 1998.

This volume rests on the assumption that a "stereoscopic view" of the Bible—its message being understood through the eyes of women as well as men—has been lacking in previous commentaries. It represents "the first comprehensive attempt to gather some of the fruits of feminist scholarship on each book of the Bible" (p. xv). Background essays and short commentaries are provided by women scholars. Bibliographies are brief.

116. Walton, John H., et al., eds. *The IVP Bible Background Commentary. Old Testament.* Downers Grove, Ill.: InterVarsity Press, 2000.

Begins with a very good general bibliography, and continues with an introductory essay to each of the sections of the Old Testament, and historical and cultural overviews of moderate length on each of the books. As with the companion New Testament volume, the main contribution of this work is to shed light on historical, archaeological, and cultural detail that is otherwise difficult to track down. Glossary, maps, charts, and indexes round out the volume.

Commentary Series

117. Albright, W. F., and David Noel Freedman, eds. Anchor Bible. Garden City, N.Y.: Doubleday, 1964–.

The most expansive commentary currently available in English. Includes volumes on the Apocrypha and accompanying reference volumes. Emphasis not only on translation but on reconstructing ancient settings. As might be expected in such an extended series, the usefulness of individual volumes is varied. (Electronic edition available.)

118. Hubbard, D. A., et al., eds. Word Biblical Commentary. Waco: Word; Nashville: Nelson, 1982–2002.

This series offers new translations and a multifaceted approach. Each section of the commentary includes bibliography, a new translation, notes, discussion of form, structure, and setting, and an "explanation." This format, which will be ideal for some and cumbersome for others, at least has the merit of breadth and variety. The theological perspective of the series could be described broadly as "conservative Protestant."

119. The International Critical Commentary. Edinburgh: T. & T. Clark, 1896–.

     No series in English has been more diligent in providing as many aids to exegesis as possible, including linguistic, textual, archaeological, and historical backgrounds. Unfortunately, most of the original series are close to a century old, and few have been updated or replaced.

120. Interpretation: A Bible Commentary for Teaching and Preaching. Louisville: John Knox, 1982–.

     While not ignoring these endeavors, this series takes less interest in exegetical, historical, and grammatical considerations than in the formulation of an interpretation of the text. In other words, exposition is of paramount concern, and so this is a strong series for those involved in preaching. Based on the Revised Standard Version and, since its appearance, the New Revised Standard Version.

121. Keck, Leander, ed. The New Interpreter's Bible. 12 vols. Nashville: Abingdon, 1994–2002.

     Few commentary series were so widely used as the original Interpreter's Bible, which appeared a half-century ago. A first, overview volume is devoted to general introductory articles, and introductions to sections of the Bible are interspersed throughout the other volumes. Short bibliographies accompany each commentary. The full texts and critical notes of two Bible translations (NIV and NRSV) are included. Generally the commentary's interest is in the received text rather than in detailed textual criticism.

122. Koester, Helmut, et al., eds. Hermeneia. Minneapolis: Fortress, 1971–.

     This series provides a "critical and historical commentary to the Bible without arbitrary limits in size or scope." More than most series, this one takes an interest in textual criticism, history of religions, etc. To be used to its potential, Hermeneia requires familiarity with biblical languages. Some of the volumes are English translations of German works, and this has implications for the accessibility of some of the extensive bibliographies.

123. New International Commentary. Grand Rapids: Eerdmans, 1959–.

     Combining a broadly conservative approach with high-level exegesis, this series (still incomplete for the Old Testament) is used frequently by pastors. Volumes are gradually being revised or replaced.

124. Oden, Thomas, et al., eds. Ancient Christian Commentary on Scripture. Downers Grove, Ill.: InterVarsity Press, 1998–.

This series draws on the often-neglected or inaccessible biblical interpretation of the patristic period (Clement of Rome [d. 215] to John of Damascus [d. ca. 760]). For each biblical passage, a selection of comments by major patristic exegetes is provided. Because both the general editors and the compilers of the individual volumes have had to select brief comments from vast bodies of patristic commentary, there is a sense in which this series functions as an *anthology* of commentary, rather than as a commentary proper. Still, the accomplishment of recovering even a selection of this tradition of commentary from near oblivion is of great value.

Chapter 4

The Church in History

I n the preface, I referred to the fact that the literature of theology is not distributed evenly by subject, period or geography, and that this makes it difficult for a research guide such as this one to provide equal access to fields of inquiry. This holds true for the study of church history, and it is at times a curious phenomenon to observe how the study of some periods and subjects seems to have generated more reference literature than others. The history of Christianity outside the Western, English-speaking world, as understood and written by indigenous peoples, for examples, is not yet as well known as it might be.

By contrast, the wealth of first-rate sources on the development of Christianity in the Western world continues to proliferate, and for almost any period of church history there are many good sources to choose from (e.g., several fairly recent encyclopedias on the Middle Ages). Because the present work is being composed and published within a North American setting, a separate section is included on historical sources for the church in North America.

Materials are arranged here under the following general headings:

Bibliographic and Research Sources
General Works

Biographical Sources
The Early Church
The Medieval Church
The Reformation
The Church in the Modern Era
The Church in North America

Bibliographic and Research Sources

125. Benowitz, June Melby. *Encyclopedia of American Women in Religion*. Santa Barbara: ABC-Clio, 1998.

    This volume's profiles of women (most of them previously obscure) are a welcome addition to the reference literature of religion and theology, and it offers an excellent chronology and a lengthy general bibliography as well. Entries vary in length from a few paragraphs to several pages. Some photographs (many not published elsewhere) are included. Each entry includes a bibliography, and cross-references are used extensively. Most articles are on individuals, but there are category and subject entries as well (Jews, Native Americans, etc.).

126. Bradley, James E., and Richard A. Muller. *Church History: An Introduction to Research, Reference Works, and Methods*. Grand Rapids: Eerdmans, 1995).

    An excellent primer for beginning researchers. Covers methods of research, historiography, sources, writing, etc. Very helpful bibliography on pp. 167–231.

127. González, Justo L. *Church History: An Essential Guide*. Nashville: Abingdon, 1996.

    A great reference tool for getting started in the study of church history, by a teacher in the field. Provides a minimalist overview of nine historical periods, each followed by a basic reading list.

128. Gorman, G. E., and Lyn Gorman. *Theological and Religious Reference Materials*. Vol. 2: *Systematic Theology and Church History*. Westport, Conn.: Greenwood, 1985.

    This volume includes an extended annotated bibliography on resources in church history (pp. 138–288). Though due for revision, the completeness of this resource keeps it useful.

129. Kepple, Robert J., and John R. Muether. *Reference Works for Theological Research*. 3rd ed. Lanham, Md.: University Press of America, 1992.
Church history covered on pp. 129–65. One of the great strengths of this book is the excellent annotations. Works, including periodical literature and dissertations, are arranged by topic.

General Works

130. Bromiley, Geoffrey, ed. and trans. *The Encyclopedia of Christianity*. 5 vols. projected. Grand Rapids: Eerdmans; Leiden: Brill, 1999–.
See #10.

131. de S. Cameron, Nigel M., et al., eds. *Dictionary of Scottish Church History and Theology*. Edinburgh: T. & T. Clark; Downers Grove, Ill.: InterVarsity Press, 1993.
Containing mostly brief entries, this work charts the development of Christianity in Scotland by documenting the ideas, events, and persons who played a part in the story. Most of the articles are associated (not surprisingly) with the Reformed churches in Scotland, though the editors have endeavored to have the volume reflect other traditions as well. Entries include bibliographies.

132. Chadwick, Owen. *A History of Christianity*. London: Weidenfeld and Nicolson; New York: St. Martin's, 1995.
A fine overview history, richly illustrated with color plates. Includes further readings, chronology, and index.

133. Cross, F. L., and E. A. Livingstone, eds. *The Oxford Dictionary of the Christian Church*. 3rd ed. London and New York: Oxford University Press, 1997.
See #3.

134. Douglas, J. D., ed. *The New International Dictionary of the Christian Church*. Rev. ed. Grand Rapids: Zondervan, 1974.
This volume's range is not nearly as broad as the *Oxford Dictionary of the Christian Church* (#3), and is in need of an update. Only the longer entries include bibliographies, and these are generally short. The use of cross-references is extensive and helpful.

135. Dowley, Tim, ed. *The History of Christianity*. A Lion Handbook. Batavia, Ill.: Lion, 1996.
Here is an unusual instance of a volume in which the visual content (which is extraordinarily good) makes a contribution at least as

important as the textual content, which tends toward quick overviews. The combination of text and illustration is very effective. There are several indexes.

136. Livingstone, E. A., ed. *The Concise Oxford Dictionary of the Christian Church*. 2nd ed. Oxford: Oxford University Press, 2000.
Like Oxford's *Concise Encyclopedia of Christianity* (#138), this is a useful source for quick reference, when no information other than the basic facts are required. Based on the 3rd edition (1997) of the authoritative *Oxford Dictionary of the Christian Church* (#3).

137. McManners, John, ed. *The Oxford Illustrated History of Christianity*. New York: Oxford University Press, 1990.
This volume incorporates a collection of 19 introductory essays by distinguished scholars (e.g., Kallistos Ware on Eastern Christendom) on Christianity through history. The combination of these essays with a superb collection of illustrations makes it an especially valuable resource for teaching. An excellent general bibliography of about 20 pages, a chronology, and an index complete the work.

138. Parrinder, Geoffrey. *A Concise Encyclopedia of Christianity*. Oxford: Oneworld Pub., 1998.
A very good quick-reference source, when one wants only the information rather than a point of departure for further research. Indexes, tables, and chronology are all helpful.

139. Schaff, Philip. *History of the Christian Church*. 8 vols. Reprint Grand Rapids: Eerdmans, 1988.
A panoramic history written at such a high level that it is still worthwhile a century after its appearance. Few works encompass such great learning and insight. Citations in Latin, German, and English are numerous within the text. Indexes of names and topics are appended to each volume.

Biographical Sources

140. Benowitz, June Melby. *Encyclopedia of American Women in Religion*. Santa Barbara: ABC-Clio, 1998.
See #125.

141. Blevins, Carolyn DeArmond, ed. *Women in Christian History: A Bibliography*. Macon, Ga.: Mercer University Press, 1995.

A short and excellent bibliographic resource, grouping entries by historical period, national/ethnic groups, denominations, etc., and adding headings for hymn writers and social reform/social work. Annotations are concise. An index of names is included.

142. Bowden, Henry W., ed. *Dictionary of American Religious Biography*. 2nd ed. Westport, Conn.: Greenwood, 1993.

A standard source for brief summaries of the lives of more than 500 American religious figures, from all periods and from a broad range of religious traditions. Bibliographic resources accompany each entry. Appendices organize the entries by denominational affiliation and birthplace. There is also a general selected bibliography and an index.

143. Cohn-Sherbok, Lavinia. *Who's Who in Christianity*. New York: Routledge, 1998.

Includes concise entries with enough bibliographic resources to enable those who want more extensive information to pursue it. Glossary, various categorical lists, and a short general bibliography are also useful.

144. Douglas, J. D., ed. *Twentieth-Century Dictionary of Christian Biography*. Grand Rapids: Baker, 1995.

This work offers short but vivid entries on Christians of the 20th century. Most are less than a page in length. The entries do a good job of noting the major writings of those whose profiles are included, but the dearth of references to other biographical sources places this volume best in the quick-reference category.

145. Lewis, Donald M., ed. *The Blackwell Dictionary of Evangelical Biography, 1730–1860*. 2 vols. Oxford: Blackwell, 1995.

This work establishes a biographical point of departure for many figures who would otherwise be completely obscure. The scope of the dictionary is broad, including figures as diverse as Samuel Johnson and David Brainerd, and most entries include some bibliographical sources.

146. Walsh, Michael, ed. *Dictionary of Christian Biography*. Collegeville, Minn.: Liturgical Press, 2001.

Brief biographies of more than 6,500 Christians. This work has attempted to include more women, and more non-Western figures, than has been the case with many earlier volumes of this kind. Entries are short, and so this resource serves best for quick reference. There is a bibliography, and indexes by dates and places of death.

The Early Church

147. Bercot, David W., ed. *A Dictionary of Early Christian Beliefs: A Reference Guide to More Than 700 Topics Discussed by the Early Church Fathers.* Peabody, Mass.: Hendrickson, 1998.

    A creative and useful resource for students who are new to the field. The author's preface provides an outline of what is unique about the period, and an opening "Who's Who" identifies the key figures. The dictionary's 700 entries will provide ready information on key topics. Cross-references abound.

148. Di Beradino, Angelo, ed. *Encyclopedia of the Early Church.* 2 vols. New York: Oxford University Press, 1992.

    An English translation of an earlier Italian work, with updated bibliographies. Covers the period up to Bede in the West and John of Damascus in the East.

149. Döpp, Siegmar, and Wilhelm Geerlings, eds. *Dictionary of Early Christian Literature.* New York: Crossroad, 2000.

    An English translation and revision of the German *Lexicon der antiken christlichen Literatur.* Bibliographic resources abound, though it should be noted that few of them are in English. An index of names is helpful.

150. Ferguson, Everett, ed. *Encyclopedia of Early Christianity.* 2nd ed. 2 vols. New York: Garland, 1997.

    This fine work includes more than 1,200 articles, written by more than 150 contributors. Textual content and excellent illustrations balance one another well. Excellent bibliographies accompany each entry, and a helpful time line is at the beginning.

151. Kadel, Andrew. *Matrology: A Bibliography of Writings by Christian Women from the First to the Fifteenth Centuries.* New York: Continuum, 1995.

    This work's objective is "to list every Christian woman who wrote before 1500 C.E., and her writings that have appeared in print since 1800" (p. 16). As such, it has addressed directly a common oversight in the bibliography of early Christian literature. Kadel provides a cursory sketch of each author, and then itemizes sources where that author's works are available in various languages. Includes bibliography and index.

152. Kelly, Joseph F. *The Concise Dictionary of Early Christianity.* Collegeville, Minn.: Liturgical Press, 1992.

    This is a very useful quick-reference source, with entries no longer than a few sentences. The A–Z entries are followed by helpful summaries of early church history, the early popes, and the Roman emperors. A short general bibliography provides the means for research in greater detail.

153. Klauck, Hans-Josef. *The Religious Context of Early Christianity: A Guide to Graeco-Roman Religions*. Edinburgh: T. & T. Clark, 2000.

An excellent portal to the abundant background literature on the diverse socioreligious milieu (mystery cults, astrology, emperor and ruler worship, etc.) in which Christianity began and eventually thrived.

154. Quasten, Johannes, ed. *Patrology*. 4 vols. Reprint. Westminster, Md.: Christian Classics, 1992.

This is a patristic collection of manageable size, with outstanding introductory materials, helpful structure and commentaries, and superb bibliographies. The editor's intended audience is the English-reading public, and (at the time its publication began in 1950) a priority was to incorporate recent advances and discoveries (e.g., texts from Egypt) into an introduction to patristic literature.

155. Robertson, Alexander, and James Donaldson, eds. *The Ante-Nicene Fathers*. Schaff, Philip, ed. *The Nicene and Post-Nicene Fathers . . . Translations of the Writings of the Fathers down to A.D. 325*. Reprint Grand Rapids: Eerdmans, 1986–1989.

The most complete English translation available of the patristic texts. (Also accessible in electronic format at http://www.ccel.org.)

156. Robinson, Thomas A., with Brent D. Shaw. *The Early Church: An Annotated Bibliography of Literature in English*. ATLA Bibliography Series 33. Metuchen, N.J.: Scarecrow, 1993.

Brings a huge array of the best literature in the field within reach of the student. Each section is introduced with a survey essay, and the annotations are thorough.

157. Young, Frances. *From Nicaea to Chalcedon: A Guide to the Literature and Its Background*. Philadelphia: Fortress, 1983.

Perhaps the strongest feature of this work is its superb two-part bibliography (pp. 333ff.), the first of which presents works in English, the second covering works in a variety of languages since 1960. The rest of the book provides a fine survey of the period A.D. 325–451.

The Medieval Church

158. *The Cambridge Medieval History*. 2nd ed. 9 vols. Cambridge: Cambridge University Press, 1966–.

This first edition of this series was launched in 1911 and was intended as a comprehensive account of medieval times. Each chapter is written by a separate author. There are full bibliographies with every chapter, and maps at the end of each volume. Though now dated, the detail and references to other literature retain a useful place for this set.

159. Cantor, Norman F., ed. *The Encyclopedia of the Middle Ages*. New York: Penguin, 1999.

   This is decidedly an *illustrated* encyclopedia: the color plates throughout the work make it a pleasure to peruse. The editor's introductory essay is helpful, as are the general index and the extensive cross-references. It is highly unusual for a work of this caliber not to include a bibliography: its inclusion would have made this work even more useful.

160. Gritsch, Eric W. *Encyclopedia of the Middle Ages*. New York: Facts on File, 1995.

   A useful work for the general reader. Includes a helpful chronology at the outset, appendices on medieval rulers of Europe, dynasties and rulers of medieval Islam, a glossary of terms, a suggested reading list, and bibliography, all in addition to 461 pages of illustrated entries A–Z.

161. *The New Cambridge Medieval History*. 7 vols. Cambridge: Cambridge University Press, 1995.

   Like its predecessor, this work is a carefully arranged collection of scholarly essays on various subjects and periods by first-rate scholars. Thus meant to be dipped into rather than read as a whole. For the bibliographies alone, there is no better starting point in English.

162. Vauchez, André, ed. *Encyclopedia of the Middle Ages*. 2 vols. Cambridge: J. Clarke; Chicago: Fitzroy Dearborn, 2000.

   This sizable work incorporates approximately 3,200 articles by some 600 scholars. Extensive black-and-white and color illustrations are included throughout. Although this translation is based on the French and Italian editions, it has been revised to include some new entries and to add some English citations to the generous bibliographies that accompany the articles. Maps, tables, and indexes are included.

The Reformation

163. Bainton, Roland H., and Eric W. Gritsch. *Bibliography of the Continental Reformation: Materials Available in English*. 2nd ed. Hamden, Conn.: Archon, 1972.

Even though this bibliography is now dated, many of the sources are of enduring interest. The topical arrangement is thorough and accessible. If used in conjunction with more recent sources, this bibliography can still be extremely helpful.

164. Baker, Derek. *The Bibliography of the Reform, 1450–1648, Relating to the United Kingdom and Ireland for the Years 1955–1970.* Oxford: Blackwell, 1975.

Here is another instance of a bibliography that is dated, but since it was quite complete up to its time it still serves as a useful component for developing a bibliography. The author provides separate bibliographies for England and Wales, Scotland, and Ireland, and under each of these headings sources are divided according to type of publication.

165. Bray, Gerald, ed. *Documents of the English Reformation.* Minneapolis: Fortress, 1994.

In a similar fashion to Lindberg's more recent work (#170), Bray presents excerpts (in Latin and English) of what was being said and written as the English Reformation unfolded. The appendices provide lists of monarchs, popes, calendars, and comparisons among key confessional documents.

166. Carney, Jo Eldridge, ed. *Renaissance and Reformation 1500–1620: A Biographical Dictionary.* Westport, Conn.: Greenwood, 2001.

This work exemplifies a balance between the quick-reference approach and a more ambitious dictionary. Concise treatments of the major figures of the period A–Z are accompanied by brief citations of works for further reading. Appendices group subjects by discipline and country. A chronology, a general bibliography, and an index are included.

167. Greengrass, Mark. *The Longman Companion to the European Reformation, c. 1500–1618.* New York: Longman, 1998.

An unusual and intelligent collection grouping research information by topic and theme, e.g., "Reactions to the Reformation" (pp. 116–70). Appendices also excellent: biographical sketches, glossary, genealogical tables, and a guide to further reading.

168. Hillerbrand, Hans J., ed. *Historical Dictionary of the Reformation and Counter-Reformation.* Lockham, Md.: Scarecrow, 2000.

Provides ready reference on key subjects and a separate bibliography at the conclusion (pp. 221–65).

169. ———, ed. *The Oxford Encyclopedia of the Reformation.* 4 vols. New York: Oxford University Press, 1996.

An invaluable resource, for the caliber of its contributors and articles, its comprehensiveness, and its helpful bibliographies (mostly in English). Essays are generous in length and, while written at a level within reach of the general reader, interact with broader academic scholarship, referred to in the bibliographies.

170. Lindberg, Carter, ed. *The European Reformations Sourcebook.* Oxford: Blackwell, 2000.
Under fourteen sequential sections, Lindberg groups together an anthology of excerpts of "who was saying/writing what" at various points during the Reformation. As such, it provides a superb means of access to primary literature that otherwise could prove unwieldy. All sources are cited fully in an appendix. There is also a fine general bibliography on pp. 282–85.

171. Maltby, William S., ed. *Reformation Europe: A Guide to Research: II.* St. Louis: Center for Reformation Research, 1992.
This volume uses the same format as its predecessor (#174), setting out scholarly essays on a given Reformation topic, each putting the bibliographic resources in context. Topics in this volume are balanced between major figures (Luther, Calvin, Zwingli) and some areas of more recent scholarly interest (cities, studies of women, family, and gender). An index of names is included.

172. Mowat, C. L., ed. *The Cambridge Modern History.* 14 vols. Cambridge: Cambridge University Press, 1958.
This venerable series follows the same format as the *Cambridge Medieval History* (##158, 161) in mapping out a comprehensive outline and then assigning major chapters within this framework (e.g., "The Ottoman Conquest") to outstanding scholars. The bibliographies for these chapters are grouped together at the conclusion of each volume. (Example: the bibliographies for vol. 1 amount to 100 pages.) A general index is included in each volume.

173. Noll, Mark, ed. *Confessions and Catechisms of the Reformation.* Grand Rapids: Baker, 1991.
This anthology sets out ten critical documents of the Reformation period (Ninety-five Theses, Thirty-nine Articles, etc.). Each of these documents is framed by an introductory essay and a list for further reading.

174. Ozment, Steven, ed. *Reformation Europe: A Guide to Research.* St. Louis: Center for Reformation Research, 1982.

This volume and its sequel (#171) provide an excellent introduction to the literature of the study of the Reformation. Sixteen topical essays introduce a specific body of literature. Subjects include the obvious (Luther) as well as more integrative approaches ("Pamphlet Literature of the German Reformation"). A general index is included.

175. Williams, George H. *The Radical Reformation.* Philadelphia: Westminster, 1963.

This volume from the Library of Christian Classics series remains an outstanding source for its thorough notes and citations. The 32 chapters cover the rise of Anabaptism in immense historical detail. The thoroughness of the indexes (Scripture as well as topics-persons-places) make the scholarship in this book readily accessible.

The Church in the Modern Era

176. *The New Cambridge Modern History.* 2nd ed. Cambridge: Cambridge University Press, 1990–.

This series is at present in a hybrid condition, with new and updated volumes still gradually appearing. Like other sets under the Cambridge imprint, this one begins with a general introductory essay. Succeeding chapters are the work of individual scholars (e.g., "The Papacy and the Catholic Church"). The consolidation of all the bibliographic resources to one concluding volume is less convenient than the practice of appending bibliographies to their respective chapters. Still, wherever the editors place them, the bibliographies in all the Cambridge series are outstanding. Each volume has its own general index.

The Church in North America

Atlases

177. Carroll, Bret E. *The Routledge Historical Atlas of Religion in America.* New York and London: Routledge, 2000.

See #2.

178. Gaustad, Edwin Scott, and Philip L. Barlow. *New Historical Atlas of Religion in America.* New York: Oxford University Press, 2001.

Reaches back to the precolonial period to describe and illustrate how religious groups arrived, came into existence, and have distributed throughout America. In this instance, the text is more important than the maps themselves.

179. Newman, William M., and Peter L. Halvorson. *Atlas of American Religion: The Denominational Era, 1776–1990.* New York and Oxford: Altamira Press, 2000.

    A historical atlas, in that the text is more important than the maps and tables. A helpful and easily usable presentation of how various Christian sects have fared geographically and numerically in America.

Other Reference Works

180. Balmer, Randall H. *Encyclopedia of Evangelicalism.* Louisville: Westminster John Knox, 2002.

    An eclectic sampling of what is germane to the identity of American evangelicalism. Has the advantage of drawing from the past generation of evangelical research, but the drawback of mixing the crucial, like Gilbert Tennent, with the trivial, like Marjoe Gortner.

181. Ellis, John Tracy, and Robert Trisco. *A Guide to American Catholic History.* 2nd ed. Santa Barbara: ABC-Clio, 1982.

    Groups bibliographical citations of works relating to United States Catholic history under broad and useful headings: general works, diocesan, biographies/correspondence, religious communities, etc.

182. Glazier, Michael, and Thomas J. Shelley, eds. *The Encyclopedia of American Catholic History.* Collegeville, Minn.: Liturgical Press, 1997.

    Entries provide basic information, and the bibliographic citations that accompany them provide access to further resources. Most entries are short, but with more than 1,600 pages, a lot of topics are covered. There are some black-and-white photographs, and a general index.

183. Hardman, Keith J. *Issues in American Christianity: Primary Sources with Introductions.* Grand Rapids: Baker, 1993.

    A documentary sourcebook for the development of Christianity in America from Alexander Whitaker (1613) to Billy Graham and beyond. Each general section is provided with an introduction and basic bibliography.

184. Hill, Samuel S. *Encyclopedia of Religion in the South.* Macon, Ga.: Mercer University Press, 1984.

    A vast work (almost 900 pages) on a vast and complex subject. Entries cover persons, movements, issues, institutions, etc. The articles range from one column to several pages, and many include bibliographic references. The use of cross-references is extensive and helpful. A general index is included.

185. Krapohl, Robert H., and Charles H. Lippy. *The Evangelicals: A Historical, Thematic, and Biographical Guide.* Westport, Conn., and London: Greenwood, 1999.

This three-part work presents concise essays on the history, themes and issues, and biographical dictionary profiles of American evangelicalism. In addition to identifying and treating insightfully the main topics, the work includes superb bibliographic resources.

186. Lippy, Charles H. *Bibliography of Religion in the South.* Macon, Ga.: Mercer University Press, 1985.

Each section of this exceptional work includes an introductory overview of the given subject and its resources. While an update is needed, the work is so thorough up to its date of publication that it still demands attention.

187. ———. *Modern American Popular Religion: A Critical Assessment and Annotated Bibliography.* Westport, Conn.: Greenwood, 1996.

Annotates more than 550 sources relating to expressions of religion that transcend the activities of the church. These include self-help groups, radio and television ministries, and the arts. Annotations are unusually thorough, and there are three indexes.

188. ———, ed. *Encyclopedia of American Religions.* 6th ed. Detroit: Gale, 1999.

A much more detailed approach to the same subject treated by Mead and Hill (# 192). Introductory and historical essays put the more specific descriptions in a broader context, and provide helpful bibliographies. Well indexed.

189. ———, ed. *Twentieth-Century Shapers of American Popular Religion.* Westport, Conn.: Greenwood, 1989.

An anthology of scholarly essays on key religious figures. This work encompasses short bibliographic essays on a diverse selection of thirty religious figures in North America (at least one of the subjects, William Aberhart, was a Canadian). Each entry includes an introduction, a biographical sketch, an appraisal, a list of writings, and sources for further study. A general index is included.

190. ———, and Peter W. Williams, eds. *Encyclopedia of the American Religious Experience.* 3 vols. New York: Charles Scribner's Sons, 1988.

The overall structure of this work is expansive: the subject is mapped out under nine broad, descriptive headings (including Historiography, Jewish and Christian Traditions, Movements, American Religious Thought and Literature, etc.). Within each of these headings is a rich variety of essays by scholars who are well versed on their topics. Each essay includes a bibliography. A general index concludes the third volume.

191. Magnuson, Norris A., and William G. Travis, eds. *American Evangelicalism*, vol. 1: *An Annotated Bibliography*; vol. 2: *First Bibliographical Supplement, 1990–1996*. West Cornwall, Conn.: Locust Hill, 1997.
These two volumes cover comprehensively the literature of the study of evangelicalism up to 1996.

192. Mead, Frank S., and Samuel S. Hill. *Handbook of Denominations in the United States*. 11th ed. Nashville: Abingdon, 2001.
See #5.

193. Melton, J. Gordon, ed. *Religious Leaders of America: A Biographical Guide to Founders and Leaders of Religious Bodies, Churches, and Spiritual Groups in North America*. 2nd ed. Detroit: Gale, 1999.
This guide profiles more than 1,200 North American figures. The format is easy to use: each entry has a number, the dates and profession of the person, and (at most) a few paragraphs of description. Each entry includes a bibliography. An appendix groups entries by affiliation, and an extensive index is included.

194. Piepkorn, Arthur Carl. *Profiles in Belief: The Religious Bodies of the United States and Canada*. 4 vols. New York: Harper & Row, 1979.
An instance of a work being done so well that it remains useful a generation after its appearance. Does a fine job of breaking down larger groups, and providing a profile of each of the smaller parts. Good (though of course dated) bibliographies.

195. Queen, Edward L., et al., eds. *The Encyclopedia of American Religious History*. Rev. ed. 2 vols. New York: Facts on File, 2002.
Unlike works such as Lippy (#189) this work tackles as broad a range of subjects as possible. Its horizon is the full breadth of religion in America up to the present time. Basic bibliographies.

196. Reid, Daniel G., ed. *Dictionary of Christianity in America*. Downers Grove, Ill.: InterVarsity Press, 1990.
See #11.

197. Roof, Wade Clark, ed. *Contemporary American Religion*. 2 vols. New York: Macmillan, 2000.
Comprises more than 500 articles on contemporary religious life, with an emphasis on "lived religion," i.e., the experiential and imaginative,

as distinct from the formal, expressions of religion. This work intentionally goes well beyond the boundaries of Christian religion, to cover the breadth and diversity of the religious experience in America. Articles include excellent bibliographies, and there is an extended general index at the end of the second volume.

198. Sandeen, Ernest R., and Frederick Hale. *American Religion and Philosophy: A Guide to Informational Sources.* Detroit: Gale Research Co., 1978.

This older work covers the literature systematically, beginning with general works and then dividing source material available for specific traditions or religious groups (North American Indians, Roman Catholics, Puritanism, etc.). Indexes by author, title, and subject conclude the work.

199. Shriver, George H., and Bill J. Leonard, eds. *Encyclopedia of Religious Controversies in the United States.* Westport, Conn.: Greenwood, 1997.

An unfortunate title, which does not accurately represent the fine content of this volume. But its entries on recent figures and issues (Ralph Abernathy, Norman Vincent Peale) are among the best available. Excellent bibliographies.

200. Stone, Jon R. *A Guide to the End of the World: Popular Eschatology in America.* New York: Garland, 1993.

It is impossible to overestimate the enduring importance of this theme within conservative Christianity, and this bibliography covers its historical development and literature admirably. An introductory essay provides background discussion of the theme, a second major section maps out the literature of American millennialism, and the final segment provides brief biographical sketches of key figures. An author index is included.

201. Williamson, William B., ed. *An Encyclopedia of Religions in the United States: One Hundred Religious Groups Speak for Themselves.* New York: Crossroad, 1992.

Based on extended interviews, this work allows religious groups to describe themselves, their history, their leaders, what makes them unique, and their contributions. Especially in the case of newer religious movements (e.g., Eckankar) this is invaluable. Bibliographies are uneven.

202. Wilson, John F., ed. *Church and State in America: A Bibliographical Guide.* 2 vols. Westport, Conn.: Greenwood, 1986.

This is a research guide of scholarly survey essays introducing bibliographies, in support of a topic that is of undiminished interest and attention. The approach is historical, with the 22 essays spanning the period from the colonial era to the late 20th century. A general index is included.

203. Young, Arthur P., and E. Jens Holley. *Religion and the American Experience, 1620–1900: A Bibliography of Doctoral Dissertations.* vol. 1; vol. 2: *The Twentieth Century.* Westport, Conn.: Greenwood, 1992–1994.
     Helpfully groups dissertations by denominations and movements, as well as by topic. Author and subject indexes conclude each volume. (Researchers should also consult *Dissertation Abstracts.*)

Chapter 5

Christian Thought and Theology

R eference sources in the discipline of theology range from the very broad (dictionaries) to the very specific (books and bibliographies relating to one specific theological issue or discussion). It is certainly true that since the first edition of *The Literature of Theology* both the range of issues being discussed and the variety of communities participating in the discussion have changed remarkably (witness the number of top-level reference sources relating to feminist theology, for example). In considering theology as an extended, ongoing discussion, as well as a field of study and research, it is worth mentioning a genre of literature that I have included only sparingly in the list to follow. Works such as the *Cambridge Companion* series (now numbering more than forty titles) are recommended for students who wish to read up-to-date scholarly essays on aspects of the thought of a certain theologian (there are volumes on Barth, Bonhoeffer, Heidegger, Kierkegaard, Ockham, etc.) or on a certain theological issue (e.g., liberation theology) provide a ready means of listening in to discussions at a very high level by some of the most distinguished theological minds of our time.

The diverse nature of current theological activity does not accommodate easy organization, and I have thought it best to organize resources in this field as follows:

Theological Terms and Vocabulary
History of Doctrine
Theology in the Contemporary Context
Dictionaries and Encyclopedias
Biographies of Theologians
Facets of Theology

Theological Terms and Vocabulary

204. McKim, Donald K. *Westminster Dictionary of Theological Terms.* Louisville: Westminster John Knox, 1996.

The language of theology is complex and diverse, and clarity of discourse requires a degree of precision. This book concisely covers almost 6,000 terms, and offers ready reference to those who want to read with understanding and write and speak with clarity. A list of works consulted concludes the volume.

205. Muller, Richard A. *Dictionary of Latin and Greek Theological Terms: Drawn Principally from Protestant Scholastic Theology.* Grand Rapids: Baker, 1985.

This book will be invaluable to anyone whose studies bring them into contact with Latin and Greek but who do not know the languages. The author has done a good job of providing definitions of just the right length, apparently reasoning that students who do not know Latin or Greek want to deal with both as little as possible in referring to a work of this kind. An index to key terms concludes the work.

206. Pelikan, Jaroslav. *The Melody of Theology: A Philosophical Dictionary.* Cambridge: Harvard University Press, 1988.

Neither a simple dictionary of terms nor a theological dictionary proper, this work is a literary exposition of concepts and themes that are timeless within theological discussion. This book is meant to foster reflection rather than furnish quick definitions.

History of Doctrine

207. Charry, Ellen T., ed. *Inquiring After God: Classic and Contemporary Readings.* Malden, Mass., and Oxford: Blackwell, 2000.

An anthology from the reflections of more than thirty Christians (ranging from Augustine to Anselm to John Paul II) in the pursuit of understanding God. It serves as "an attempt to help readers learn to think better theologically so that they may see what Christian claims . . . actually entail" (p. xviii). Each of the selections is placed in context with an introduction, and is followed by a reflection written by a contemporary theologian and some bibliographic notes.

208. Douglas, J. D., Walter A. Elwell, and Peter Toon. *The Concise Dictionary of the Christian Tradition: Doctrine, Liturgy, History.* Grand Rapids: Regency Reference Library, 1989.
    A quick-reference source, with entries providing only basic facts and dates.

209. Evans, G. R. *The Medieval Theologians.* Oxford: Blackwell, 2001.
    This work includes overview essays by a variety of contributors on 22 theologians from Augustine to Wycliffe, grouped under six general historical headings. The emphasis is on providing a general outline of the life, setting, and thought of each, rather than citing extensively from the theologians themselves. Each of the essays has its own notes and reading list. A general index is included.

210. Hart, Trevor A., ed. *The Dictionary of Historical Theology.* Carlisle, Cumbria, UK; Waynesboro, Ga.: Paternoster; Grand Rapids: Eerdmans, 2000. See #13.

Theology in the Contemporary Context

Bibliography

211. Thorsen, Don. *Theological Resources for Ministry: A Bibliography of Works in Theological Studies.* Nappanee, Ind.: Evangel, 1998.
    This work illustrates vividly the difference between a book list and an annotated bibliography. As a representative of the former category, it does a commendable job of itemizing what is available. An annotated work would have been of far more use as an evaluative and comparative tool for the scholar.

Other Sources

212. Ford, David F., ed. *The Modern Theologians: An Introduction to Christian Theology in the Twentieth Century.* 2nd ed. Cambridge, Mass.: Blackwell, 1997.
    A major work of 36 chapters and almost 800 pages, covering the modern theological landscape comprehensively. Only about a third of the essays are devoted to individual theologians; the bulk of the work is given to schools, approaches, and regions, and this serves the task better than a more biographical approach. Introductions to the various

sections are instructive, bibliographies and notes for each essay are extensive, and a list of dates, glossary, and index round out the work. An indispensable guide to the subject.

213. Gunton, Colin E., ed. *The Cambridge Companion to Christian Doctrine.* Cambridge, UK; New York: Cambridge University Press, 1997.
     Fourteen essays by major theological writers on major theological themes of our time. This volume provides a helpful means of gaining exposure to the primary interests of Christian theology at the present time. The opening pages include a glossary and a chronology. Each essay includes extensive notes and a list for further reading. A general index is included.

214. Hastings, Adrian, et al., eds. *The Oxford Companion to Christian Thought.* Oxford: Oxford University Press, 2000.
     See #14.

215. McGrath, Alister E., ed. *The Blackwell Encyclopedia of Modern Christian Thought.* Cambridge, Mass.: Blackwell, 1993.
     See #15.

216. O'Collins, Gerald, and Edward G. Farrugia. *The Modern Theologians: An Introduction to Christian Theology in the Twentieth Century.* New York: Paulist, 2000.
     This volume falls somewhere between a dictionary of terms and a brief dictionary: a kind of theological phrase book. Useful to those who are either entirely new to theological language or who find themselves in conversation with unfamiliar theological communities.

Dictionaries and Encyclopedias

217. Byrne, Peter, and Leslie Houlden, eds. *Companion Encyclopedia of Theology.* London; New York: Routledge, 1995.
     A useful companion, but not an encyclopedia. Forty-eight articles, arranged in six sections. Any of these articles, each with its own bibliography, could provide a good starting point for research on the respective topics.

218. Elwell, Walter A., ed. *The Concise Evangelical Dictionary of Theology.* Abridged by Peter Toon. Grand Rapids: Baker, 1991.
     Basic definitions of terms, movements, events, persons, and ideas. An abridgment of the earlier *Baker's Dictionary of Theology.* The function

of a work like this is to provide ready access to definitions and summaries in those instances where more detailed study is not the objective. Cross-references are used extensively and effectively.

219. ———. *Evangelical Dictionary of Theology.* 2nd ed. Grand Rapids: Baker, 2001.

There are about 1,200 entries, from roughly 200 contributors, in this work of about 1,200 pages. Only the longer articles (e.g., "Image of God") include bibliographic recommendations. The work is informed by a conservative evangelical framework, and this results in a lot of attention to Scripture. Articles are devoted to themes and doctrines, persons, denominations, schools of thought, controversies, etc., in an evenhanded manner.

220. Ferguson, Sinclair B., David F. Wright, and J. I. Packer, eds. *New Dictionary of Theology.* Leicester, England; Downers Grove, Ill.: InterVarsity Press, 1988.

Numerous entries characterize this sizable work (738 pp., double columns). Basic bibliographies accompany most articles. A good combination of a ready-reference and a starting-point tool for research.

221. Komonchak, Joseph A., et al., eds. *The New Dictionary of Theology.* Wilmington, Del.: Glazier, 1987.

As noted in the preface, this is "the first collaborative attempt to take stock of the remarkable developments in the [Catholic] church and in theology since the [Vatican II] Council" (p. v). Articles include bibliographies.

222. Richardson, Alan, and John S. Bowden, eds. *The Westminster Dictionary of Christian Theology.* Philadelphia: Westminster, 1983.

A quick-reference source for introductory information on theological topics. Entries are mostly brief, but enough citations are included to provide a next step for students who wish to take it.

Biographies of Theologians

223. Carey, Patrick W., and Joseph T. Lienhard, eds. *Biographical Dictionary of Christian Theologians.* Westport, Conn.: Greenwood, 2000.

Entries of medium length (with bibliographies) on more than 450 theologians. A very good ready-reference source for historical summaries, especially for those figures who are not widely known. Includes a brief general bibliography and an index.

224. Elwell, Walter A., ed. *Handbook of Evangelical Theologians*. Grand Rapids: Baker, 1993.

    An anthology of sketches that provide a sense of the cultural and theological milieu in which these scholars worked. The list of theologians profiled here suggests an eclectic definition of "evangelical," as many of the figures differed greatly in matters of ecclesiology, style, and practice.

225. Ford, David F., ed. *The Modern Theologians: An Introduction to Christian Theology in the Twentieth Century*. 2nd ed. Cambridge, Mass.: Blackwell, 1997.

    See #212.

226. Musser, Donald W., and Joseph L. Price, eds. *A New Handbook of Christian Theologians*. Nashville: Abingdon, 1996.

    See #16

227. O'Collins, Gerald, and Edward G. Farrugia. *The Modern Theologians: An Introduction to Christian Theology in the Twentieth Century*. New York: Paulist, 2000.

    See #216.

228. Peerman, Dean G., and Martin E. Marty, eds. *A Handbook of Christian Theologians*. Nashville: Abingdon, 1984.

    Sketches and overviews of major theologians from Schleiermacher to Küng. This book serves as a very good quick-reference source, with minimal space given to bibliography or indexes. One unique strength of this volume is the distinguished combinations of contributors and subjects: Richard Niebuhr on Schleiermacher, Pauck on Harnack, Braaten on Pannenberg, etc. Articles are arranged under broad headings, in historical rather than alphabetical sequence.

Facets of Theology

Theological Traditions

Protestant

229. Beeke, Joel R. *A Reader's Guide to Reformed Literature: An Annotated Bibliography of Reformed Theology*. Grand Rapids: Reformation Heritage Books, 2001.

    In less than 100 pages, the author arranges a wealth of citations, grouped in correspondence with the 37 articles of the Belgic Confession of Faith (1531). This structure proves to be logical, innovative, and effective.

230. ———, and Sinclair B. Ferguson. *Reformed Confessions Harmonized.* Grand Rapids: Baker, 1999.
A parallel "harmony" of seven major Reformed confessions (Heidelberg, Westminster, Dort, etc.). The editors provide a historical introduction.

231. Johnson, William Stacy, and John H. Leith, eds. *Reformed Reader: A Sourcebook in Christian Theology.* 2 vols. Louisville: Westminster/John Knox, 1993.
A well-edited anthology of excerpts from the Reformation to 1788 (vol. 1) and from 1799 to the present (vol. 2). Each volume uses the same broad structure to illustrate what Reformation and Reformed thinkers have written on the major themes of theology. Bibliographies are interspersed throughout, and each volume has its own index.

Roman Catholic

232. Beinert, Wolfgang, and Francis Schüssler Fiorenza, eds. *Handbook of Catholic Theology.* New York: Crossroad, 1995.
The English edition of *Lexikon der katholischen Dogmatik* (1987). Covers major themes in considerable depth, and the articles are accompanied by bibliographies, mostly of works in English.

233. Glazier, Michael, and Monika K. Hellwig, eds. *The Modern Catholic Encyclopedia.* Collegeville, Minn.: Liturgical Press, 1994.
An extensive (931 pages) general-purpose treatment of the major Catholic themes. The articles tend to be short, with no bibliographies, but helpful cross-references are used throughout. An alphabetical listing of entries is included at the beginning, and there are some illustrations.

234. Hardon, John A. *Modern Catholic Dictionary.* Garden City, N.Y.: Doubleday, 1980.
This is a fine one-volume reference source for general information. The dictionary itself runs through key topics A–Z, and the appendix ably includes quick-reference resources such as lists of popes, Roman and Byzantine calendars, and lists of communities and institutes.

235. McBrien, Richard P., ed. *The HarperCollins Encyclopedia of Catholicism.* New York: HarperCollins, 1995.
At well over 1,000 pages, this work not only covers more topics, and at greater length, than related reference works (such as 234, above), but also includes longer feature articles (e.g., Aquinas, Augustine, monasticism, etc.). Accompanied by illustrations (maps, color plates, drawings); many entries include bibliographies.

236. Neuner, J., and J. Dupuis, eds. *The Christian Faith in the Doctrinal Documents of the Catholic Church.* New York: Alba House, 1990.

     A sourcebook, gathering excerpts of historical Catholic thought and decrees to illustrate the development of doctrine and teaching up to the present time. Commentary is limited. Includes chronology and indexes.

237. O'Donnell, Christopher. *Ecclesia: A Theological Encyclopedia of the Church.* Collegeville, Minn.: Liturgical Press, 1996.

     This work deliberately attempts to avoid duplicating topics that have been covered already by other Catholic publications (such as #235, above), and focuses on theological issues specifically relating to the church, its history, etc. Notes are extensive.

238. Rahner, Karl, ed. *Encyclopedia of Theology: The Concise Sacramentum Mundi.* Reprint. New York: Seabury, 1986.

     A distillation of the core content of the six-volume postconciliar *Sacramentum Mundi.* Even this abridgment is still about 1,800 densely packed pages, and so is still to be considered a major Catholic encyclopedia in its own right. Though the articles are written at a scholarly level, in this abridgment the bibliographies are omitted.

239. Shaw, Russell, ed. *Our Sunday Visitor's Encyclopedia of Catholic Doctrine.* Huntington, Ind.: Our Sunday Visitor Pub., 1997.

     Essentially an enlargement on the 1992 *Catechism of the Catholic Church* (cf. #436). This survey volume strikes a reasonable balance between scholarly and popular coverage of a wide variety of subjects. Bibliographies accompany the longer articles, and a general index is included.

Eastern Orthodox

240. Day, Peter D. *The Liturgical Dictionary of Eastern Christianity.* Collegeville, Minn.: Liturgical Press, 1993.

     A handbook for those to whom worship in the Orthodox tradition is completely foreign. Entries are succinct, and are further simplified by a quick-reference guide, as well as by tables comparing the practices and terminology of Alexandrine, Antiochene, Byzantine, etc., traditions.

241. Demetrakopoulos, George H. *Dictionary of Orthodox Theology: A Summary of the Beliefs, Practices and History of the Eastern Orthodox Church.* New York: Philosophical Library, 1964.

     A quick-reference source, written at a time when interest in the Orthodox tradition had not yet attained its current level in North America.

242. Litsas, Fotios K., ed. *A Companion to the Greek Orthodox Church: Essays and References.* New York: Department of Communication, Greek Orthodox Archdiocese of North and South America, 1984.

    For those requiring a one-volume introduction to a tradition unknown to them, this would provide the ideal point of entry, including essays on history, sacraments, calendar, art and architecture, etc. Appendices include a time line, lists of Patriarchs of Constantinople, etc.

243. Parry, Ken, et al., eds. *The Blackwell Dictionary of Eastern Christianity.* Oxford, UK; Malden, Mass.: Blackwell, 1999.

    For a one-volume work, this dictionary covers a lot of ground, encompassing almost 700 entries, by 50 contributors, covering history, theology, liturgy, etc. Many articles include brief bibliographies, and there is an expansive concluding index. Particularly for one who is an outsider to the Orthodox tradition, this volume is one of the most useful resources available in English.

244. Patrinacos, Nicon D. *A Dictionary of Greek Orthodoxy.* Pleasantville, N.Y.: Hellenic Heritage Pub., 1984.

    A general reference work covering the essential themes, ideas, and figures of Greek Orthodoxy. Though it does include a basic index, there are no bibliographic resources. Illustrations are placed in the margins. An appendix provides concise information on important names mentioned in the text.

245. Prokurat, Michael, et al. *Historical Dictionary of the Orthodox Church.* Lanham, Md.: Scarecrow, 1996.

    In addition to a helpful general introduction, and a concise A–Z treatment of topics and themes (with special emphasis on the period from 1850 on), this work contains an outstanding bibliography of almost 100 pages (pp. 349ff.).

Theological Topics

Ethics and Theology

246. Atkinson, David J., and David H. Fields, eds. *New Dictionary of Christian Ethics and Pastoral Theology.* Downers Grove, Ill.: InterVarsity Press, 1995.

    An impressive, two-part work. First, a selection of 18 primary themes in this field are treated in essays; second, shorter topics are covered in the remaining 700+ pages. In both sections, articles have good bibliographies.

247. Becker, Lawrence, and Charlotte B. Becker, eds. *Encyclopedia of Ethics.* 2nd ed. 3 vols. New York: Garland, 2001.

A comprehensive resource, with almost 600 substantial articles on every imaginable subject relating to ethics. The articles include fine bibliographies, and so this work can provide the ideal starting point for broader study on a great many subjects. The concluding volume provides extensive subject and citation indexes.

248. Carman, John, and Mark Juergensmeyer, eds. *A Bibliographic Guide to the Comparative Study of Ethics.* Cambridge and New York: Cambridge University Press, 1991.

The title does not quite do this work justice: introductory essays to each chapter by subject specialists contribute at least as much to the work as the bibliographic content. Among other chapters (on Hinduism, etc.) are four chapters on Christian ethics (early, medieval, Reformation, and modern). The annotations throughout are excellent.

249. Childress, James F., and John Macquarrie, eds. *The Westminster Dictionary of Christian Ethics.* Philadelphia: Westminster, 1986.

This work offers thorough coverage of the field in an A-Z sequence, encompassing articles within the broad areas of Basic Ethics, Biblical Ethics, Theological Ethics, Philosophical Ethical Traditions (Kant, etc.), Non-Christian Religious Ethics (Buddhism, etc.), and Ethical Problems. Most of the articles are compact, and some come with short bibliographies. A name index is provided.

250. Clarke, Paul Berry, and Andrew Linzey, eds. *Dictionary of Ethics, Theology and Society.* London and New York: Routledge, 1996.

The aim of this work is to identify and describe the major ethical, theological, and political influences in Western society. A scholarly work, with copious bibliographies accompanying the articles. (Example: Thomas Torrance on "Capitalism," pp. 105–10.) Includes a general index.

251. Harrison, R. K., ed. *Encyclopedia of Biblical and Christian Ethics.* Rev. ed. Nashville: Nelson, 1992.

This work is intended to serve as a reference work for the general user, or for a student who requires a basic background for ethical reflection and/or research on a given aspect of Christian ethics. Its entries are generally concise, and bibliographic notes are frequent. Cross-references are used extensively. (Example: the article on "Marriage" has cross-references to those on "Family" and "Procreation.")

252. Terkel, Susan Neiburg, and R. Shannon Duval, eds. *Encyclopedia of Ethics.* New York: Facts on File, 1999.

This concise one-volume approach presents a clear alternative to #247. Here is offered quick-reference material, definitions, etc. Five pages of general bibliography and a general index are included.

253. Wogaman, J. Philip, and Douglas M. Strong, eds. *Readings in Christian Ethics: A Historical Sourcebook.* Louisville: Westminster John Knox, 1996.

This helpful anthology brings together excerpts from writings on ethical subjects from the tradition of the church, beginning with Clement and continuing up to the present time. Includes a subject index.

Feminist Theology

254. Carson, Anne. *Feminist Spirituality and the Feminine Divine: An Annotated Bibliography.* Trumansburg, N.Y.: Crossing Press, 1986.

Of only marginal relevance to the Christian theological enterprise, but instructive as an indicator of the extent to which theological concepts such as "divine" have been reconstituted in current discourse.

255. ———. *Goddesses & Wise Women: The Literature of Feminist Spirituality, 1980–1992: An Annotated Bibliography.* Freedom, Calif: Crossing Press, 1992.

Though this bibliography's religious interests are quite diffuse, it does includes one section (pp. 154–77) on "Christianity and Judaism: Woman-Centered Re-Visioning." A brief subject index concludes this volume.

256. Finson, Shelley David, ed. *Women and Religion: A Bibliographic Guide to Christian Feminist Liberation Theology.* Toronto: University of Toronto Press, 1995.

Here is a helpful guide to the literature, organized under recognizable headings such as "Bible," "Ministry," "Pastoral Care," "Spirituality," etc. It is not clear whether—within the enterprise of mapping out needed reference sources in religion—the sequestering of a body of contemporary religious writing within such familiar topics will prove to be of sustained value. But in the process of mapping out a developing field of theological inquiry, it is quite useful. This volume concludes with an extensive index.

257. Fischer, Clare Benedicks. *Of Spirituality: A Feminist Perspective.* Evanston, Ill.: American Theological Library Association; Lanham, Md.: Scarecrow, 1995.

Documents the common ground between the literatures of spirituality (broadly defined) and feminism. Resources are grouped under broad headings.

258. ———, and Dorothea McEwan, eds. *An A to Z of Feminist Theology.* Sheffield: Sheffield Academic Press, 1996.

    As the name implies, a topical dictionary, and though individual entries are interesting, it is hard to see how an alphabetical approach is the ideal template: an entry on an established theological concept such as "grace" in the same volume as an entry on "Greenham Common Women's Peace Camp"? To be fair, it could be maintained that these are the kinds of editorial tensions that are unique to a branch of theological inquiry still in its formative stages. Few bibliographic resources accompany entries, and the concluding bibliography is uneven in quality.

259. Russell, Letty M., and J. Shannon Clarkson, eds. *Dictionary of Feminist Theologies.* Louisville: Westminster John Knox, 1996.

    A well-arranged and edited A–Z introductory approach to the field. Individual entries have their own bibliographic resources, and there is a fine general bibliography of about 25 pages at the conclusion.

260. Walsh, Mary-Paula. *Feminism and Christian Tradition: An Annotated Bibliography and Critical Introduction to the Literature.* Westport, Conn.: Greenwood, 1999.

    At almost 500 pages, and with unusually detailed annotations, this work provides an outstanding access point to a growing and uneven body of literature. Walsh's 30 pages of introduction, and multiple indexes, make this an even stronger source.

261. Young, Serinity, ed. *An Anthology of Sacred Texts by and about Women.* New York: Crossroad, 1993.

    This collection uses a world religions approach, offering selections from Judaism, Hinduism, Buddhism, Shamanism, and other traditions in addition to Christianity. Each of the sections on these themes concludes with an extended bibliography. Individual subject essays are introduced by brief overviews, which are quite helpful. This volume includes subject and name indexes.

262. ———, ed. *Encyclopedia of Women and World Religion.* 2 vols. New York: Macmillan, 2000.

    The purpose of this distinguished work is to serve as a "culturally and historically comprehensive reference work that reflects contemporary approaches to women's history and experience in world religion" (p. vii). Most entries are fairly lengthy, with helpful bibliographies.

Liberation Theology

263. Davis, Thomas J., ed. *Liberation Theology: A Bibliography Selected from the ATLA Religion Database.* Chicago: American Theological Library Association, 1985.

Like other ATLA printed bibliographies, this one was generated by an electronic search. An impressive list of citations is included. The work is presented in separate subject and author-title lists.

264. Musto, Ronald G. *Liberation Theologies: A Research Guide.* New York: Garland, 1991.

Employs a very broad definition of "liberation theologies," including not only the standard categories (Bible, church history, theology, etc.) but also African, black, feminist, etc., theologies. The annotations are uneven, and (because of lack of clear topical definition) could have benefited from editorial intervention.

265. Rowland, Christopher, ed. *The Cambridge Companion to Liberation Theology.* Cambridge and New York: Cambridge University Press, 1999.

Follows the standard format for volumes in this series by providing an introductory essay, then a selection of further essays on the topic grouped within major themes ("Contemporary Liberation Theology," "Aspects of Liberation Theology," "Analysis and Criticism"). In addition to the endnotes for each essay, there is a select bibliography and index at the end.

Theology in the African American Context

266. DuPree, Sherry Sherrod. *African-American Holiness Pentecostal Movement: An Annotated Bibliography.* New York: Garland, 1996.

A fine example of how one bibliographer's work can almost single-handedly bring a field of research into manageable condition. In this comprehensive, 650-page volume, there are sections on existing bibliographic sources, Pentecostal history, various subgroups within Pentecostalism, founders and leaders, etc. The annotations are extensive. The appendices include a glossary, lists of denominations, and addresses of sources. A comprehensive and a geographical index complete the volume.

267. Evans, James H. *Black Theology: A Critical Assessment and Annotated Bibliography.* New York: Greenwood, 1987.

An introductory essay outlines the subject, and the bibliography groups the literature under "Origins," "Main Currents," and "Cultural-Global

68   *Christian Thought and Theology*

Discourse." The annotations in this work are exceptionally thorough. There is a need for an update. Three indexes conclude this work.

268. Jones, Charles Edwin. *Black Holiness: A Guide to the Study of Black Partici- pation in Wesleyan Perfectionist and Glossolalic Pentecostal Movements.* Metuchen, N.J.: Scarecrow, 1987.

The subject is divided into four broad groupings: "Black Holiness," "Wesleyan-Arminian Orientation," "Finished Work of Calvary Orien- tation," and "Leader-Centered Orientation." To students who are accustomed to more commonplace subject divisions than these, the lengthy index at the book's conclusion may be especially helpful. A sec- tion on schools is included, as is one on biography.

269. Murphy, Larry G., et al., eds. *Encyclopedia of African American Religions.* New York: Garland, 1993.

The A–Z subject treatment (many of the entries are probably not cov- ered by other reference books) is preceded by three lengthy introduc- tory essays on religion in the African American community, on the influence of Martin Luther King, and on womanist theology within the African American community. Of particular value is the "Basic Bibli- ography of African American Religion" on pages 865ff. Directories and indexes are included.

270. Payne, Wardell J., ed. *Directory of African American Religious Bodies: A Com- pendium by the Howard University School of Divinity.* Washington, D.C.: Howard University Press, 1995.

A complete directory, supported by well-crafted scholarly essays that provide background and historical overviews. Religious bodies are divided by denomination, and sketches of African American centers of religious education are included. There are excellent bibliographies and indexes.

271. Richardson, Marilyn. *Black Women and Religion: A Bibliography.* Boston: G. K. Hall, 1980.

A thoughtful and well-presented contribution. The bibliography is introduced by a sketch of three women in the black church, illustrat- ing the need for this kind of literature to be better known and more accessible. Annotated citations are grouped under general headings of Literature, Music, Art, etc.

272. Salzman, Jack, David Lionel Smith, and Cornel West, eds. *Encyclopedia of African-American Culture and History.* 5 vols. New York: Macmillan Library Reference, 1996.

A major work that includes many articles of religious and theological interest (e.g., "Black Theology," by James Cone). The incorporation of illustrations and bibliographies along with the text itself is very effective (e.g., "Spirituals" in vol. 5, pp. 2551–53). The appendices and indexes to this source are exceptionally thorough, and will facilitate searching the contents of this sizable work.

273. Williams, Ethel L., and Clifton F. Brown. *The Howard University Bibliography of African and Afro-American Religious Studies: With Locations in American Libraries.* Wilmington, Del.: Scholarly Resources, 1977.
    A fine example of "what bibliographic technology could offer" a generation ago: a compendious, database-generated printout of a bibliography in a field acutely underserved by library resources. The utility and versatility of this excellent resource would be multiplied if it were offered in an electronically searchable format.

274. Young, Josiah U. *African Theology: A Critical Analysis and Annotated Bibliography.* Westport, Conn.: Greenwood, 1993.
    There is not enough literature to support good research in this field, and this volume may be the best point of entry for acquiring a general grasp and for initiating further study.. Annotations in the second part are detailed, indexes are extensive.

Hispanic Theology

275. Barton, Paul, and David Maldonado, eds. *Hispanic Christianity within Mainline Protestant Traditions: A Bibliography.* Decatur, Ga.: Asociación para la Educación Teológica Hispana, 1998.
    The work is divided by the traditional areas of theological education (Theology, Bible, etc.). Each is introduced by a scholar in the field. A reference work of this caliber is likely to improve markedly the awareness and use of this body of literature.

Non-Western Theologies

276. Fabella, Virginia, and R. S. Sugirtharajah, eds. *Dictionary of Third World Theologies.* Maryknoll, N.Y.: Orbis, 2000.
    This work represents the first attempt to systematize non-Western theology that originates largely from outside the West. Put differently, it attempts to avoid having Western scholars inventory and explain Third World theologies to the people of the Third World church. Uneven in its treatment of different subjects, but subsequent editions are bound to mature.

Apologetics

277. Geisler, Norman L. *Baker Encyclopedia of Christian Apologetics.* Grand
      Rapids: Baker, 1999.
      There is a dearth of reference resources in this field. Though in this
      work it is not always clear why a given subject has a particularly apolo-
      getic relevance, the coverage is at least thorough. It is unusual to see an
      encyclopedia that is the work of one author. Both the sources for indi-
      vidual articles and the general bibliography at the end are outstanding.

278. Latourelle, René, and Rino Fisichella, eds. *Dictionary of Fundamental The-
      ology.* New York: Crossroad, 1994.
      English translation of the Italian *Dizzionario di Téologia Fondamentale*
      (1990). Whatever it may connote in Italian, the appellation "Funda-
      mental" is problematic in a North American setting: what is meant is
      foundational, with a strong element of apologetics. The organization is
      unusual, with the index at the beginning. But the essays come from a
      broad range of distinguished contributors, and the bibliographies that
      accompany the entries are extensive.

Christology

279. Hultgren, Arland J. *New Testament Christology: A Critical Assessment and
      Annotated Bibliography.* New York: Greenwood, 1988.
      This work introduces the subject in terms of various recent approaches
      to christological study, and uses these contours as a means of organiz-
      ing the literature (Foundations, Titles, Themes, etc.). The opening
      chapter, which surveys the recent literature, provides a useful backdrop
      to the rest of the book's contents. Most of the annotations are detailed;
      indexes by name, title, and subject are included.

Apocalypticism

280. McIver, Tom. *The End of the World: An Annotated Bibliography.* Jefferson,
      N.C., and London: McFarland, 1999.
      More than 3,500 works are cited, many with lengthy annotations,
      arranged in four historical periods from pre-1800 up to the present
      time. The index alone runs to more than fifty pages.

The Holy Spirit

281. Mills, Watson E. *A Bibliography of the Nature and Role of the Holy Spirit in
      Twentieth-Century Writings.* Lewiston, N.Y.: Mellen Biblical Press, 1993.
      Though the title appears at first glance to describe a narrow subject,
      this work presents almost 4,000 entries (without annotations). Many of
      the entries are from "popular" publications. Well indexed.

282. Schandorff, Esther Dech. *Doctrine of the Holy Spirit: A Bibliography Show-ing Its Chronological Development.* 2 vols. Lanham, Md.: American Theo-logical Library Association and Scarecrow, 1995.

A work of astounding thoroughness, covering almost 7,000 entries on the subject. Volume 1 lists the entries alphabetically, vol. 2 by subject. If there is a weakness, it is that the nature and value of the literature in this realm is so uneven that the work's exhaustiveness may prove an encumbrance.

Ecology

283. Sheldon, Joseph Kenneth. *Rediscovery of Creation: A Bibliographical Study of the Church's Response to the Environmental Crisis.* Metuchen, N.J.: Scare-crow, 1992.

When the interest of the church turns rather suddenly toward a previ-ously neglected subject or issue, it is difficult to keep track of what is being written and by whom. This bibliography is an example of such an endeavor. Needs to be updated, but useful up to its date of publication.

The Problem of Evil

284. Whitney, Barry L. *Theodicy: An Annotated Bibliography on the Problem of Evil, 1960–1991.* Bowling Green, Ohio: Philosophy Documentation Cen-ter, Bowling Green University, 1998.

The first part of this work maps out with some precision the variety of possible recent ways to account for the "problem of evil." Of the sev-eral appendices, one surveys theodicy in historical theology, and another provides an outline of some of the current miscellaneous pub-lications in this field. An extremely useful resource for any scholar hav-ing a sustained interest in this major theological theme.

The Church and the World

285. Wolcott, Roger T., and Dorita F. Bolger. *Church and Social Action: A Crit-ical Assessment and Bibliographical Survey.* New York: Greenwood, 1990.

An introductory essay provides an overview of the challenges and methodology for researching the present topic. The five main chapters outline resources on Religion in Modern Society, Survey Research and Organizational Studies, Religious Social Movements—United States, Comparative Studies, and Historical Studies. There are three indexes.

Family, Sexuality, and Theology

286. Ecker, Ronald L. *And Adam Knew Eve: A Dictionary of Sex in the Bible.* Palatka, Fla.: Hodge and Braddock, 1995.

Though not as systematic as it could have been, this work attempts to explore sexuality as presented by biblical events and teachings. The subjects treated in this A–Z approach range from the obvious to the very obscure. A general bibliography and author and title index are included.

287. Hisel, Lisa M., ed. *Sexuality and Christianity: A Bibliography Focusing on the Catholic Experience*. Washington, D.C.: Catholics for a Free Choice, 1998.
     A basic topical list of citations, grouped under general headings ("Contraception," "Celibacy," etc.). A helpful feature of this brief work is its inclusion of a section identifying primary church documents.

288. Leston, Douglas R., ed. *Sex and Marriage in the Catholic Tradition: A Historical Overview*. Ottawa, Ont.: Novalis, 2001.
     A sourcebook of writings on the subject from Aristotle to the present. No introductions are provided for the 51 selections, but a bibliography is included for each. A list of sources is included at the conclusion.

289. Melton, J. Gordon. *The Churches Speak on Homosexuality*. Detroit: Gale Research, 1991.
     This unique work draws from a quarterly monograph series titled The Churches Speak, which coordinates official church positions on various contemporary issues, in this case homosexuality. Statements were solicited by The Churches Speak by means of a mailing to every North American religious body with more than 100,000 members. Allowing for the fact that the 1990s was a decade when debate and policy on the subject shifted considerably, this volume still provides a one-of-a-kind snapshot of what various (mostly Christian) communities were thinking. The statements are prefaced by an introductory essay on "The Churches' Ethical Dilemma with Homosexuality," which includes a helpful bibliography. A good general index concludes the volume.

290. ———. *The Churches Speak on Sex and Family Life: Official Statements from Religious Bodies and Ecumenical Organizations*. Detroit and London: Gale Research, 1991.
     An introductory essay by Nicholas Piediscalzi addresses "The Changing Vision of Sexuality and the Family." The remainder of the volume arranges statements on this subject from various religious communions: Catholic, Protestant and Eastern Orthodox, Jewish groups, and other religious bodies. As such, it serves as a sourcebook for reading on the extent to which religious views on this subject have changed (or remained unchanged) in recent years. A basic index is provided.

Heresy, Heterodoxy

291. George, Leonard. *Crimes of Perception: An Encyclopedia of Heresies and Heretics.* New York: Paragon House, 1995.

Two resources are provided in this book: first, the introductory material charts the psychology and phenomenon of heresy (what it means, how it is understood in its time and over time). Second, of course, there is an encyclopedia of entries carefully arranged by topic. Example: an entry on "Doukhobors" (pp. 100–101) describes the genesis of this sect in eastern Europe of the 18th century, early leadership, the later support from Tolstoy, and large-scale immigration to Canada in the early 20th century.

Chapter 6

World Christianity, Ecumenics, and World Religions

The study of globalization from a historical, theological, and ethical perspective has been one factor contributing to change in the way Christian missions are understood. One welcome result of this in recent years has been a great surge of interest in the study of Christianity as a world religion by historians and missions scholars. The quantity and caliber of reference sources in this sector has increased dramatically, perhaps best illustrated by the second edition of the *World Christian Encyclopedia* (#294).

Reference literature for the study of ecumenism is more limited and is not expanding significantly at present. But the available resources—including a bibliography, a historical dictionary, and an encyclopedia—are very good, so the subject is reasonably well served.

By contrast, if there is one conspicuous area of the study of religion and theology to find a publishing surplus, it is in world religions. The shelves of many libraries groan under the weight of shelves full of bulky, phonebook-sized reference volumes, all of them good in their way, but covering a lot of heavily traveled terrain. I have included a substantial selection of these below. The related subject of new religious movements is less stable (and therefore more difficult to profile definitively in reference books), but the literature is energetic, fascinating, and in constant need of updating.

Selections are arranged under the following categories:

World Christianity
Ecumenics
World Religions

World Christianity

Statistics and Almanacs

292. *The Almanac of the Christian World.* Wheaton, Ill.: Tyndale House, 1990–.
     A helpful utilization of the "world almanac" format to the Christian scene, including sections such as "The Year in Review," "Organizations and Foundations," etc. A good source for quick reference and fact checking.

293. Barrett, David B., and Todd M. Johnson, eds. *World Christian Trends, AD 30–AD 2200: Interpreting the Annual Christian Megacensus.* Pasadena: William Carey Library, 2001.
     This colossus of statistical information (almost 1,000 oversize pages) is energized in part by a sharp tension (articulated in the preface) between two traditions of describing the scope of Christianity in the world: the approaches of comparative religions and of Christian missions. A work of these dimensions can be explained only by an explosion of statistical data that has been harvested through the circulation of 10 million questionnaires annually (the "megacensus"). The introduction describes the process involved, and the succeeding sections cover the history, data, methods, analysis, and strategy associated with the project. A final section (reference) provides a glossary, bibliography (20 pages, 600 entries), indexes, and geoatlas.

Handbooks and Encyclopedias

294. Barrett, David B., George T. Kurian, and Todd M. Johnson, eds. *World Christian Encyclopedia: A Comparative Survey of Churches and Religions in the Modern World.* 2nd ed., 2 vols. New York: Oxford University Press, 2001.
     See #1.

295. Brierley, P. W., ed. *World Churches Handbook.* London: Christian Research, 1997.
     This is an outstanding statistical guide to worldwide Christianity. Figures for the entire world are presented first, and the rest of the volume provides data by country A–Z. Separate tables are included for "Non-

Trinitarian" groups (Jehovah's Witnesses, etc.). Tables for each country outline population, total members by denomination, "other churches," "non-Trinitarian groups," etc. A general index is provided. Unlike #293, this volume offers almost no narrative or interpretation.

296. Siewert, John A., and Edna G. Valdez, eds. *Mission Handbook, 1998–2000.* 17th ed. Monrovia, Calif.: MARC, 1997.

Eleven chapters outline the current state of world mission activity and provide current information on mission agencies. The volume is the outgrowth of a statistical survey, and the questionnaire itself is included among several other appendices. Tables and graphs visualize the statistical content.

Other Sources

297. Anderson, Gerald H., ed. *Biographical Dictionary of Christian Missions.* New York: Macmillan Reference USA, 1998.

A superb source of biographical information, bringing together some 2,400 entries, adding up to a "who's who" in the history of the expansion of Christianity. Includes bibliographies, indexes, and useful groupings of entries (e.g., "martyrs") in appendices.

298. Dwight, Henry Otis, et al., eds. *The Encyclopedia of Missions: Descriptive, Historical, Biographical, Statistical.* 2nd ed. Reprint. Detroit: Gale Research, 1975.

Originally published in 1891, this work is now primarily of interest for historical purposes. A rich source of information, with mostly short entries, and appendices providing chronological and statistical tables, etc.

299. Moreau, A. Scott, gen. ed. *Evangelical Dictionary of World Missions.* Grand Rapids: Baker, 2000.

More than 1,400 entries. Provides an up-to-date overview of mission ideas, practices, history, etc., compiled by evangelical scholars. Articles include their own bibliographies. At more than 1,000 pages, the coverage is quite thorough. A "Master Outline" at the back of the book provides an alternate means of navigating this volume.

300. Müller, Karl, et al., eds. *Dictionary of Mission: Theology, History, Perspectives.* Maryknoll, N.Y.: Orbis, 1997.

An English translation and revision of *Lexikon Missionstheologischer Grundbegriffe.* Articles of substantial length outline the basic concepts of mission theology. Articles include extensive bibliographies.

301. Neill, Stephen, Gerald H. Anderson, and John Goodwin, eds. *Concise Dictionary of the Christian World Mission.* Nashville and New York: Abingdon, 1971.
     Covers the extension of the Christian church from 1492. Most entries are short, and include at least some bibliographic resources.

302. Pate, Larry. *From Every People: A Handbook of Two-Thirds World Missions with Directory/Histories/Analysis.* Monrovia, Calif.: MARC, 1989.
     Puts a conceptual grasp of the enterprise of world missions into a convenient form. Analysis of which groups are active and where, illustrated with numerous charts and graphs.

303. Petersen, Paul D., ed. *Missions and Evangelism: A Bibliography Selected from the ATLA Religion Database.* Chicago: American Theological Library Association, 1985.
     A colossal bibliographic resource, indexed by subject and author/editor. Needs to be updated in order to remain useful.

304. Siewert, John A., and Edna G. Valdez, eds. *Mission Handbook 1998–2000: U.S. and Canadian Christian Ministries Overseas.* Monrovia, Calif.: MARC, 1997.
     See #296.

305. Thomas, Norman E., ed. *Classic Texts in Mission & World Christianity.* Maryknoll, N.Y.: Orbis, 1995.
     A well-selected and well-presented anthology of historical Christian thought on the mission of the church in the world. Covers the field from the early church (*Letter to Diognetus*) to the contemporary period (Moltmann, etc.).

Atlases

306. Brierley, P. W., and Heather Wraight. *Atlas of World Christianity: 2000 Years.* Nashville: Nelson, 1998.
     Basic statistical and analytical data on the church in history, in its missionary activity, by continent, presented in an attractive graphic format.

307. Dowley, Tim, ed. *Atlas of the Bible and Christianity.* Grand Rapids: Baker, 1997.
     See #4.

Ecumenics

308. Fahey, Michael A. *Ecumenism: A Bibliographical Overview.* Westport, Conn.: Greenwood, 1992.

The perfect starting point for anyone wanting to investigate ecumenical writings and documentation. This guide gathers sources under general themes such as historical accounts, bilateral dialogues, doctrinal issues, etc.

309. Lossky, Nicholas, ed. *Dictionary of the Ecumenical Movement.* Grand Rapids: Eerdmans, 1991.

At more than 1,000 pages, this work covers the ecumenical landscape in some detail with articles (including bibliographies) of varying length. Well-indexed and illustrated, includes bibliographies.

310. Van der Bent, Ans Joachim. *Historical Dictionary of Ecumenical Christianity.* Metuchen, N.J.: Scarecrow, 1994.

Beginning with a general chronology and introductory essay, this work covers a broad range of subjects including people, events, documents, etc. The articles themselves do not include bibliographies, but a separate bibliography is included at the end (pp. 529–95).

311. World Council of Churches. *World Council of Churches: Yearbook.* Geneva: World Council of Churches Publications, 1995–.

An annual volume descriptive of the structure, activity, and functions of the WCC, as well as an overview of WCC work in the year previous.

World Religions

Atlases

312. Halvorson, Peter L. *Atlas of Religious Change in America, 1952–1990.* Atlanta: Glenmary Research Center, 1994.

This work provides graphic representation of statistical shifts in religious populations at a level of detail that extends all the way to counties. Maps are arranged alphabetically by denomination, with one section for each decade covered. Textual summaries accompany the maps, which are well presented and easy to use.

313. Smart, Ninian, ed. *Atlas of the World's Religions.* New York: Oxford University Press, 1999.

A rich combination of text, glossary, bibliography, charts, maps, and color illustrations all represent vividly the rich diversity of global religious life and expression.

New Religious Movements

314. Barrett, David V. *Sects, 'Cults,' and Alternative Religions: A World Survey and Sourcebook.* London: Blandford, 1996.

Covers the field in five broad sections: historical background, religious groups with Christian origins, groups with Eastern origins, esoteric and neo-pagan movements, and psychology and self-help groups. Includes extensive endnotes, a directory, general bibliography, and index.

315. Brasher, Brenda E., ed. *Encyclopedia of Fundamentalism.* New York and London: Routledge, 2001.

This work resists categorization: though its brief introduction attempts clarification of *Christian* fundamentalism, there are other entries included on "Entertainment Industry," "Islamic Fundamentalism," "Mormons, Fundamentalist," etc. The overall result is somewhat unwieldy. This work includes mostly longer articles, each with its own bibliography. There are some illustrations and an extended index.

316. Chryssides, George D. *Historical Dictionary of New Religious Movements.* Lanham, Md.: Scarecrow, 2001.

Like the other volumes in this fine series (Historical Dictionaries of Religions, Philosophies, and Movements), this one provides three things: a concise introductory survey to the field, a dictionary of brief entries, and an extensive bibliography (including Websites) of about 130 pages. The contents are very well indexed.

317. Lewis, James R. *Peculiar Prophets: A Biographical Dictionary of New Religions.* St. Paul: Paragon House, 1999.

The author's definition of "new religions" might raise a few eyebrows (J. Gresham Machen gets an entry across the page from Shirley MacLaine). This work includes brief sketches on more than 350 figures, mostly from the 20th century. While the entries themselves lack bibliographies, there is a good general bibliography of more than 100 pages (297–400). Some illustrations.

318. ———, ed. *The Encyclopedia of Cults, Sects, and New Religions.* Amherst, N.Y.: Prometheus, 1998.

Everything from the Duck River (and Kindred) Association of Baptists to Heaven's Gate to the Teutonic Temple are covered in brief articles. There are some illustrations, and a superb bibliography of more than 60 pages at the conclusion.

319. Mather, George A., and Larry A. Nichols. *Dictionary of Cults, Sects, Religions and the Occult.* Grand Rapids: Zondervan, 1993.

This work represents a somewhat more apologetic approach than is seen in other works on contemporary religions, offering good general overviews of many diverse religious groups. There are several appendices (ecumenical creeds of Christendom, christological heresies, a list of groups treated in this volume, and influences/antecedents of various groups) and a good general bibliography.

320. Turner, Harold W. *Bibliography of New Religious Movements in Primal Societies.* 2 vols. Boston: G. K. Hall, 1977.
These volumes provide extensive bibliographic resources on black African and North American religious movements, respectively. Annotations are brief but useful. Indexes of authors and titles are extensive. While now dated, this work is important, as some of these fields of study are still poorly represented in the literature.

World Religions

321. Adams, Charles J., ed. *A Reader's Guide to the Great Religions.* New York: Free Press, 1977.
Though in need of updating, this volume brings together the best bibliographic resources for study of the major religious traditions. The bibliographies are each introduced by the scholar-specialist who compiled them. Author and subject indexes are included.

322. Alexander, Pat, ed. *Eerdmans Handbook to the World's Religions.* Rev. ed. Grand Rapids: Eerdmans, 1994.
This book offers a quick-reference alternative to its massive counterparts, combining short entries with fine illustrations. The overall approach is historical, beginning with the development of religion, and progressing to ancient religions, primal religions, etc. A "Rapid Fact-Finder" offers a micro-version of the book, with quick summaries (in tiny typeface): helpful to those for whom "quick reference" is not "quick" enough.

323. Bowker, John, ed. *The Concise Oxford Dictionary of World Religions.* Oxford: Oxford University Press, 2000.
This "concise" version has reduced the number of entries of #324. Bowker's fifteen-page introductory essay provides a background for the consideration of the individual subjects that follow. A lengthy index helps to facilitate access.

324. ———, ed. *The Oxford Dictionary of World Religions.* Oxford: Oxford University Press, 1997.
The main strength of this volume is its comprehensiveness: 1,000 pages including more than 8,000 entries. The longer entries include bibliographies. A thorough topic index is included.

325. ———, ed. *World Religions.* New York: DK Pub., 1997.
This work offers a sumptuous 200-page gallery illustrating the life and symbols of the major religions of the world. The chapters include concise introductions, and extensive notes accompany the color plates. Time lines, maps, and a bibliography round out this vivid work.

326. Doniger, Wendy, ed. *Merriam-Webster's Encyclopedia of World Religions.* Springfield, Mass.: Merriam-Webster, 1999.
This volume is a terrific combination of short articles and (where called for) longer entries on the major topics within the field. Topical collections of superb color plates are interspersed throughout. A fine bibliography is included. Lacks only an index.

327. Earhart, H. Byron, ed. *Religious Traditions of the World: A Journey Through Africa, Mesoamerica, North America, Judaism, Christianity, Islam, Hinduism, China, and Japan.* New York: HarperCollins, 1993.
An outstanding textbook on world religions. Each of the ten lengthy chapters includes a chronology, an introduction, an overview of the religious cultures of a given region or tradition, a summary, study questions, notes, glossary, and a reading list. This volume of more than 1,200 pages serves as an authoritative guide to the subject. In some cases (native religions of North America) the book does an especially fine job of putting the subject in a broader religious studies context.

328. Eliade, Mircea, ed. *The Encyclopedia of Religion.* 16 vols. New York: Macmillan, 1987.
This work is the definitive resource in English. The examples are of scholarly depth and scope but are not written in an excessively technical style. (Example: "Afro-American Religions," by Albert J. Raboteau, runs to six pages, including a historical overview and separate major sections on Christian and Muslim traditions, each with its own fine bibliography.) A concluding volume offers an alphabetical list of entries, a synoptic outline of contents, and a thorough index.

329. Eliade, Mircea, Ioan P. Culianu, and Hillary S. Weisner. *The Eliade Guide to World Religions.* San Francisco: HarperSanFrancisco, 1991.
A well-designed source offering quick definitions, brief outlines, and sources for further reading. All the major world religious groups are covered in about 300 pages.

330. Ellwood, Robert S. *The Encyclopedia of World Religions.* New York: Facts on File, 1998.

This fine general reference source combines short articles with black-and-white illustrations, topical outline, basic bibliography (including a few electronic resources), and index. The entries are of moderate length (e.g., "Mecca, Pilgrimage to," is covered in about two columns), and provide a good starting point for further research.

331. Harris, Ian, et al., eds. *Contemporary Religions: A World Guide.* Harlow, UK: Longmans, 1992.

Part I includes overview essays by established scholars (e.g., Ninian Smart) on the major religious traditions (with basic bibliographies), Part II is an A–Z listing of brief summaries of religious groups and movements, and Part III is an alphabetical country-by-country summary. There is also a glossary and name index. This work is a good source for quick profiles of the religious life of a given country.

332. Hinnells, John R., ed. *A New Handbook of Living Religions.* Cambridge, Mass.: Blackwell, 1997.

A collection of scholarly survey essays, in two parts: the major religions of the world, and cross-cultural issues (religion and gender, international migration). Each of these essays includes extensive endnotes. There is also a general bibliography and a detailed index. Serves admirably as a middle-level resource, between quick-reference sources and lengthy monographs.

333. ———, ed. *A New Dictionary of Religions.* Oxford: Blackwell, 1995.

The contents of this work are listed at the beginning by subject area and author: a helpful means for the reader to navigate an expansive and complex field. An excellent bibliography of 100 pages (edited by N. K. Firby) and a thorough index accompany about 600 pages of mostly brief A–Z entries.

334. ———, ed. *Who's Who of World Religions.* New York: Simon and Schuster, 1992.

Here are biographical entries on hundreds of key figures, A–Z, with an outstanding general bibliography, maps, and index. While the entries do consistently provide citations for the writings themselves within the text, they do not provide sources for further research.

335. Hirschfelder, Arlene, and Paulette Molin. *Encyclopedia of Native American Religions.* Updated ed. New York: Facts on File, 2000.

"The entries in this book cover the spiritual traditions of native peoples in the United States and Canada before contact with Europeans and Americans" (p. vii). There are an excellent bibliography and a topical index at the conclusion.

336. Jenkins, Jon C., ed. *International Biographical Dictionary of Religion: An Encyclopedia of More Than 4,000 Leading Personalities.* Munich: K. G. Saur, 1994.

    Mainly a quick-reference source. Where possible, bibliographic information associated with a given person is provided. Indexes are extensive, by country, religion, organization, etc. Many if not most of the figures are obscure, quite possibly not referred to in any other reference work.

337. Lundin, G. Edward, and Anne H. Lundin, eds. *Contemporary Religious Ideas: Bibliographic Essays.* Englewood, Col.: Libraries Unlimited, 1996.

    The selection of topics treated in this work's twelve chapters is unusual: aging, church libraries and their history, alongside more obvious topics such as Islam, Jewish literature, Latin American liberation theology, etc. However, the editors have chosen contributors who know their fields well, and these contributors' introductory essays and carefully annotated bibliographies are immensely useful.

338. *Macmillan Compendium of World Religions: Selections from the Sixteen-Volume Macmillan Encyclopedia of Religion.* New York: Macmillan, 1997.

    See #18.

339. Pye, Michael, ed. *The Continuum Dictionary of Religion.* New York: Continuum, 1994.

    The function of this resource is to provide concise summary articles on key terms, concepts, institutions, and persons of world religions. Cross-references are used extensively. There is a good general bibliography.

340. Schumacher, Stephan, and Gert Woerner, eds. *The Rider Encyclopedia of Eastern Philosophy and Religion.* London: Rider, 1989. Published in the U.S. as *The Encyclopedia of Eastern Philosophy and Religion.* Boston: Shambhala, 1989.

    "Presents the basic terminology and doctrinal systems of the four great wisdom teachings of the East—Buddhism, Hinduism, Taoism, and Zen—in a clearly understandable form" (p. vii). Entries for all four areas are interspersed in the same alphabetical listing. A thorough bibliography is included for each of the four.

341. Smith, Jonathan Z., ed. *The HarperCollins Dictionary of Religion.* San Francisco: HarperSanFrancisco, 1995.

    Feature articles on the major religions, and more than 3,000 articles on shorter subjects. Though there are some illustrations, the strength of this work is its text. Lacks an index.

342. Snodgrass, Mary Ellen. *Encyclopedia of World Scriptures.* Jefferson, N.C., and London: McFarland, 2001.

A creative anthology of excerpts from religious texts through history. Description, citation, and some analysis are included. Within the limits of about 275 pages, selections are brief, yet this work is a fine execution of a very good idea for a reference book, in that it presents in one volume representative selections from a huge diversity of traditions. Includes a chronology for world scriptures and a good general bibliography.

343. Union of International Associations. *World Guide to Religious and Spiritual Organizations.* Munich: K. G. Saur, 1996.

This substantial guide provides brief descriptions, directories by country, subject, and foundation dates for about 3,500 organizations, many of them obscure. There are several appendices, providing further information on types of organizations, statistics, etc.

Chapter 7

Christian Denominations

R eaders will notice immediately that, to put it mildly, not all
Christian communities are equally well written about. It is
worth noting in passing that this is not only an inconvenience for
the interested researcher, but a tactical misfortune for the affected
Christian community. The production of critical resources that
outline the history and purpose of communities is one of the ways
in which such groups not only expand numerically but mature in
confidence in mission. A quick comparison and contrast reveals
that many of the global bodies that are the fastest growing remain
the least represented on the shelves of reference collections. The
only explanation for this is that up to now such books simply have
not been written. This of course places severe limitations on how
well scholars can understand and write about such communities,
and (worse still) on how the identity and mission of such communities can be better understood.

The citations for this chapter illustrate how bountiful resources
are available for some branches of Christendom (e.g., Roman
Catholics), and how sparse they are for others (e.g., Pentecostals
and charismatics).

Selections are arranged under the following categories:

The Protestant Tradition
The Catholic Tradition

The Eastern Orthodox Tradition
Other Traditions

The Protestant Tradition

Episcopal

344. Armentrout, Don S., and Robert Boak Slocum, eds. *Documents of Witness: A History of the Episcopal Church, 1782–1985*. New York: Church Hymnal Corporation, 1994.
    A sourcebook of literature illustrative of the development of the Episcopal Church in the U.S.A. Each of the 165 selections is given a concise introduction. A chronology is added as an appendix.

345. Caldwell, Sandra M., and Ronald J. Caldwell. *The History of the Episcopal Church in America, 1607–1991: A Bibliography*. New York: Garland, 1993.
    This is a thorough bibliographic resource not only for history but for various other aspects of the E.C.U.S.A. The sources are sensibly divided by type of publication ("Reference Works," "General Histories," etc.), by historical period, (more generally) by topic, etc. Although the entries are not annotated, this book's almost 4,000 entries are easily searched through a thorough index at the end.

346. *The Episcopal Church Annual*. Harrisburg: Morehouse, 2002.
    This publication serves the dual purposes of a directory of church people, parishes, institutions, and organizations and a ready-reference source for facts and information about the Episcopal Church (maps, lists of bishops, religious orders, publications, etc.).

347. Evans, G. R., and J. Robert Wright, eds. *The Anglican Tradition: A Handbook of Sources*. Minneapolis: Fortress, 1991.
    This handbook comprises an anthology of Anglican documents illustrative of the doctrinal development and tradition of Anglicanism through many centuries. Scripture and general indexes are included.

348. McGrath, Alister E., ed. *The SPCK Handbook of Anglican Theologians*. London: SPCK, 1998.
    A work in two parts: a regional survey of Anglican theology, and a survey of Anglican theologians. Bibliographies throughout. Especially valuable as a guide to the wide diversity in Anglican theology among different regions at the present time.

349. Ollard, S. L., et al. *Dictionary of English Church History*. London and Oxford: Mowbray, 1948.

Though an older work, this is still a fine source on Anglican history. (For example, an entry under "Ely, See of," provides not only information on the region and its history, but a sketch of each bishop of Ely since its establishment.)

350. Wall, John N. *A Dictionary for Episcopalians*. Cambridge: Cowley, 2001.

This work offers very basic definitions of the key vocabulary of Anglicanism (e.g., "Chrism," "Faldstool," "Ordinary Time," "Thurible"). Illustrations in black-and-white provide a helpful complement to the text. It will be of greatest benefit to non-Anglicans or to those who are new to the Episcopal communion. There is no index.

Presbyterian/Reformed

351. Bauswein, Jean-Jacques, and Lukas Vischer, eds. *The Reformed Family Worldwide: A Survey of Reformed Churches, Theological Schools, and International Organizations*. Grand Rapids: Eerdmans, 1999.

This work serves as a fact book for the global Reformed community. There are two main parts: basic historical information on the Reformed tradition, and an extended list of Reformed churches, educational institutions, and other organizations. A section of maps is included.

352. Benedetto, Robert, Darrell Guder, and Donald K. McKim. *Historical Dictionary of Reformed Churches*. Lanham, Md.: Scarecrow, 1999.

Following the format of other volumes in this series (historical dictionaries of religions, philosophies, and movements), this work presents a collection of concise entries on the figures, ideas, events, issues, etc., within the Reformed tradition. The international scope of the work is impressive. An extended chronology and introduction, as well as a major bibliography of almost 150 pages, make the dictionary still more useful and instructive.

353. Davis, Thomas J., ed. *The Reformed Traditions, 16th–19th Centuries: A Bibliography Selected from the ATLA Religion Database*. Chicago: American Theological Library Association, 1986.

A printout from a search of the electronic version of the excellent ATLA Religion Database. While the number of citations is impressive, this kind of presentation is not easy to use, in that it cannot be readily searched. The same content in more versatile formats may now be accessed through more recent CD-ROM or World Wide Web versions of this database.

354. Gasero, Russell L. *Historical Directory of the Reformed Church in America, 1628–2000.* Grand Rapids: Eerdmans, 2001.
This work provides an exhaustive index of clergy, congregations, professors, missionaries, etc., for one of North America's oldest Protestant denominations.

355. Hart, D. G., and Mark Noll, eds. *Dictionary of the Presbyterian and Reformed Tradition in America.* Downers Grove, Ill.: InterVarsity Press, 1999.
The editors' survey essay introduces almost 300 pages of entries on key ideas, persons, and events. Entries have good bibliographies. The typeface is small, but there are benefits to having such a quantity of information in a compact volume.

356. McKim, Donald K., ed. *Encyclopedia of the Reformed Faith.* Louisville: Westminster/John Knox, 1992.
Articles treating the major events, persons, ideas, and issues associated with the Reformed tradition, chiefly in the North American and Western European settings. In addition to a list of selected resources in the preface, articles present their own brief bibliographies.

357. ———, ed. *The Westminster Handbook to Reformed Theology.* Louisville: Westminster John Knox, 2001.
This volume extracts the entries on specifically theological topics from #356 and re-presents them as a reader of theological thought in the Reformed tradition. This is a creative and useful way of "re-purposing" a set of resources, and the resulting volume has the merits of being concise and focused in setting out the major terms, issues, etc., of the Reformed theological tradition. The bibliographies with each entry have been retained from the earlier volume, and a brief list of "Selected Resources" is also included.

358. Parker, Harold M. *Bibliography of Published Articles on American Presbyterianism, 1901–1980.* Westport, Conn.: Greenwood, 1985.
Historical information published in serials is often unwieldy: not all of it is indexed, and what *is* indexed is not all in the same index. Thus a work such as this one serves to bring together an extensive list in one point of access. The structure is simple: a list of almost 3,000 articles arranged alphabetically by author. A topical index is included.

359. Prince, Harold B. *A Presbyterian Bibliography: The Published Writings of Ministers who Served in the Presbyterian Church in the United States during*

Its First Hundred Years, 1861–1961, and Their Locations in Eight Significant Theological Collections in the U.S.A. Metuchen, N.J.: Scarecrow, 1983.

The subject of this bibliography is the sort of material that is notoriously difficult to access in a systematic fashion: literature by and about ministers of the Presbyterian tradition in the United States. Contains over 4,000 entries, with an index.

360. Rohls, Jan. *Reformed Confessions: Theology from Zurich to Barmen.* Louisville: Westminster John Knox, 1998.

The purpose of this volume is to study the critical confessional documents of Reformed theology, place them in a historical context, and provide comment throughout. Theological and historical reflections on the confessions to the mid-20th century are provided by the author, an esteemed professor. The work includes a bibliography and subject index.

361. Trinterud, Leonard J. *A Bibliography of American Presbyterianism During the Colonial Period.* Philadelphia: Presbyterian Historical Society, 1968.

This work brings some order and improved access to a body of material that was originally published mostly under the auspices of different synods, presbyteries, etc. Entries are in fact grouped regionally, under the title of particular synods or presbyteries. The topical index is especially useful in searching a list that represents so many different places, times, and subjects.

Lutheranism

362. Bachmann, E. Theodore, and Mercia Brenne Bachmann. *Lutheran Churches in the World: A Handbook.* Minneapolis: Augsburg, 1989.

This work needs to be updated, but is still most helpful in providing an outline of where Lutherans are in the world, and in what numbers. Material is divided by regions. A miscellany of statistics and directories is included at the end.

363. Bodensieck, Julius, ed. *The Encyclopedia of the Lutheran Church.* 3 vols. Minneapolis: Augsburg, 1965.

Though dated, this work is still of great value for its historical coverage of major issues, figures, and themes in world Lutheranism. Only selected articles have bibliographies.

364. DeBerg, Betty A. *Women and Women's Issues in North American Lutheranism.* Minneapolis: Augsburg Fortress, 1992.

A specialized bibliographic source of immediate value to those wishing to find resources relating to women and Lutheranism. (Example: the section on biographies brings together several pages of citations that, if indexed elsewhere at all, would not otherwise be presented together.)

365. Gassmann, Günther. *Historical Dictionary of Lutheranism.* Lanham, Md.: Scarecrow, 2001.
   Like other volumes in this series (Historical Dictionaries of Religions, Philosophies, and Movements), this volume offers brief entries on key ideas, persons, incidents, and themes within this tradition, accompanied by helpful statistics. An appendix maps out the variety of Lutheran bodies worldwide, and the concluding bibliography of works in English (pp. 371–417) is impressive.

366. Huber, Donald L. *World Lutheranism: A Select Bibliography for English Readers.* Lanham, Md.: Scarecrow, 2000.
   An expansive bibliography (without annotations) on the history, culture, and life of Lutheranism. Its interest in Lutheranism as a worldwide movement makes it a useful complement to #365. Succeeding chapters cover reference works, historical Lutheranism (by region), cross-cultural missions, and contemporary Lutheranism. A name index is provided.

367. Lueker, Erwin L., ed. *Lutheran Cyclopedia.* Rev. ed. St. Louis: Concordia, 1975.
   Because of its comprehensiveness, this work remains useful in spite of its date. Most entries are very short, and bibliographies accompany only the more lengthy articles. Its greatest value is as a quick-reference source.

368. Petersen, Paul D. *Luther and Lutheranism: A Bibliography Selected from the ATLA Religion Database.* Chicago: American Theological Library Association, 1985.
   Like other bibliographies that are essentially printouts from the excellent ATLA Religion Database, this one is a mixed blessing: huge in scope (861 pages) but of limited utility, in that it lacks an index. A more focused result, with the advantages of electronic searchability, can be attained through a search of the electronic version(s) of the ATLA-RDB (whether via CD-ROM or one of the Web-based presentations).

369. Wiederaenders, Robert C. *Historical Guide to Lutheran Church Bodies of North America.* 2nd ed. St. Louis: Lutheran Historical Conference, 1998.
   Primarily of use to the historian of Lutheranism who needs help unraveling the various strands of the Lutheran communion. Includes 20 pages of general Lutheran bibliography.

Methodism

370. Field, Clive D. *Bibliography of Methodist Historical Literature, 1999.* Birmingham, Eng.: Information Services, University of Birmingham, 1999.
    This work is a periodic supplement to the *Proceedings of the Wesley Historical Society*, and provides an update of publications in the field, especially within the British setting.

371. Kirby, James E., Russell E. Richey, and Kenneth E. Rowe. *The Methodists.* Westport, Conn.: Greenwood, 1996.
    Like its Congregational counterpart in this series (Denominations in America), this volume serves as an overview and sourcebook for a specific Protestant tradition. The material is arranged under four parts: Bishops, Conference, Members, and Biographical Dictionary. Each essay contains rich bibliographical citations. The concluding bibliographical essay provides useful directions for those wishing to pursue more extended study.

372. Rowe, Kenneth E. *United Methodist Studies: Basic Bibliographies.* 4th ed. Nashville: Abingdon, 1998.
    An essential guide for mapping out the bibliographic resources associated with Methodism. Includes general, historical, doctrinal, polity, periodical, and nonprint resources.

373. Yrigoyen, Charles, Jr., and Susan E. Warrick. *Historical Dictionary of Methodism.* Lanham, Md.: Scarecrow, 1996.
    A chronology and a brief history of Methodism are followed by about 250 pages of dictionary entries, mostly about a page in length. The bibliography is separate from the entries, but extensive (about 50 pages).

Pentecostal, Holiness, and Charismatic

374. Burgess, Stanley M., and Gary B. McGee, eds. *Dictionary of Pentecostal and Charismatic Movements.* Grand Rapids: Zondervan, 1989.
    Serves as a basic reference tool for the study of a group whose documentation has only recently begun to be undertaken in a satisfactory manner. Contains articles on major issues (e.g., hermeneutics) as well as on otherwise obscure figures within the movement. Needs updating, but still very useful.

375. DuPree, Sherry Sherrod. *African-American Holiness Pentecostal Movement: An Annotated Bibliography.* New York: Garland, 1996.
    See #266.

376. ———, ed. *Biographical Dictionary of African-American, Holiness-Pentecostals, 1880–1990.* Washington, D.C.: Middle Atlantic Regional Press, 1989.
Takes on a neglected but difficult area for research (documentation is unfortunately scanty). A short historical overview (pp. xi–xix) helps put the entries that follow in historical perspective. A list of obituaries, a list of dissertations, and an appendix of bibliographies conclude the volume.

377. Jones, Charles Edwin. *A Guide to the Study of the Pentecostal Movement.* 2 vols. Metuchen, N.J.: Scarecrow, 1985.
Now in need of a revision, this scholarly bibliography divides this expansive field of study into four headings: the Pentecostal Movement, Doctrinal Traditions, Schools, and Biography. The dynamic character of this movement has tended not to produce "institutionalized" or centralized publishing ventures, and this makes the work of pulling such scattered resources together all the more valuable. The index itself runs to almost 150 pages.

378. ———. *The Charismatic Movement: A Guide to the Study of Neo-Pentecostalism with Emphasis on Anglo-American Sources.* 2 vols. Metuchen, N.J.: Scarecrow, 1995.
The incredible diffuseness of subject material brought into order to compile this resource is a tribute to the perseverance that this project required. It can be considered a parallel resource to #377, using the same outline for its treatment of the subject. There are four broad parts covering the literature of the Charismatic Movement, Denominational and Organizational Responses, Schools (associated with the movement), and Biography (journal articles profiling figures within the movement). The index is extensive.

379. Kostlevy, William C., ed. *Historical Dictionary of the Holiness Movement.* Lanham, Md.: Scarecrow, 2001.
Because this movement generally is loosely organized, and because its current rate of growth is exceptionally high, this work is a timely guide to the major themes, figures, and ideas within the Holiness tradition from John Wesley onward. A chronology and a good bibliography support the A–Z subject treatment.

380. ———. *Holiness Manuscripts: A Guide to Sources Documenting the Wesleyan Holiness Movement in the United States and Canada.* Metuchen, N.J., and London: Scarecrow, 1994.
Begins with a lengthy essay on the historiography of the Holiness movement, then provides careful annotations on collections in the U.S. and Canada, with information on repositories.

381. Miller, William Charles, ed. *Holiness Works: A Bibliography*. Kansas City, Mo.: Nazarene Pub. House, 1986.
    A listing of 1,400 works in the Holiness tradition, grouped under the headings of Bibliography, Biblical, General and Theological, Sermons and Devotionals, and Testimonies. A name index is included.

Baptists

382. Brackney, William H. *The Baptists*. Westport, Conn.: Greenwood, 1994.
    An excellent guide to the study of the Baptists. Two major sections provide an outline of the Baptist tradition (history, major social and theological issues) and a biographical dictionary of Baptist leaders. The appendices include a chronology and a fifteen-page bibliographic essay.

383. ———. *Historical Dictionary of the Baptists*. Lanham, Md.: Scarecrow, 1999.
    This work begins with a chronology of Baptist history and an overview essay. The dictionary itself contains mostly brief entries on major Baptist figures, themes, and institutions. Entries do not include bibliographies, but a very good bibliography is included on pp. 465–94.

384. George, Timothy, and David S. Dockery, eds. *Baptist Theologians*. Nashville: Broadman, 1990.
    Profiles of 33 Baptist theologians, from John Bunyan to Clark Pinnock, with introductory and concluding essays by the editors. Entries are long enough to provide a good overview, and each includes its own bibliography and notes. General index.

385. Harrison, Harrold D. *Who's Who among Free Will Baptists, and Encyclopedia of Denominational Information*. Nashville: Randall House, 1978.
    About half the book is essentially a ministerial directory. The remainder comprises a series of brief histories of denominational schools, departments, committees, etc.

386. Leonard, Bill J., ed. *Dictionary of Baptists in America*. Downers Grove, Ill.: InterVarsity Press, 1994.
    Most articles of this historical dictionary include a bibliography. The editor's introduction (pp. 1–15) provides a fine historical framework for the A–Z subject coverage that follows. Articles are distributed widely, including issues, movements, persons, institutions, doctrines, etc.

387. McBeth, Leon H. *A Sourcebook for Baptist Heritage*. Nashville: Broadman, 1990.

This anthology of Baptist thought from the 17th century onward brings together excerpts from primary sources in a strategic arrangement. Each section is placed in historical context by McBeth. Statistical tables and general index are included. The historical framework and the diversity of sources cited make this an especially strong resource for teaching purposes.

388. Wardin, Albert W. *Baptist Atlas.* Nashville: Broadman, 1980.
     This older atlas presents a visual representation of the historical development of the Baptist movement, especially within the United States. It now serves mostly as an historical reference source.

Seventh-day Adventists

389. Bjorling, Joel. *The Churches of God, Seventh Day: A Bibliography.* New York: Garland, 1987.
     A thorough inventory of widely scattered publications on a poorly documented segment of Protestant Christianity. The introductions to various sections are very helpful in covering the contours of Sabbatarianism.

390. *Seventh Day Adventist Encyclopedia.* 2nd rev. ed. 2 vols. Hagerstown, Md.: Review and Herald, 1996.
     A compendium of information about the work, beliefs, organization, history, and key figures of the Seventh-day Adventists. Selective maps and charts. No bibliographies.

Congregationalism

391. Youngs, J. William T. *The Congregationalists.* Westport, Conn.: Praeger, 1998.
     This two-part work covers two broad areas: first, the history of Congregationalism (especially in North America), treated in ten essays; second, biographical profiles of the major figures of Congregationalism (e.g., Timothy Dwight). Both the essays and the profiles include their own bibliographies. A chronology and bibliographical essay are included.

Society of Friends/Quakers

392. Barbour, Hugh, and J. William Frost. *The Quakers.* Richmond, Ind.: Friends United Press, 1994.
     There are two sections to this book. In the first, a series of 21 concise essays traces the historical development of this community in England

and later in America. Each chapter includes extended notes and bibliography. The second section is a concise biographical dictionary, including a bibliographic essay.

Unitarian/Universalist

393. Robinson, David. *The Unitarians and the Universalists*. Westport, Conn., and London: Greenwood, 1985.
    The first part of this work outlines in twelve brief chapters the origins and development of this community. (There are extended endnotes at the conclusion of this section.) This is followed by a biographical dictionary of leaders, including bibliographies. A general bibliographic essay concludes the volume.

Shakers

394. Duffield, Holley Gene. *Historical Dictionary of the Shakers*. Lanham, Md., and London: Scarecrow, 2000.
    Reflecting the unique character of a diminishing rather than expanding community, this dictionary is brief and concerned almost completely with the past. A chronology precedes this dictionary, and concluding appendices include selections from foundational documents, and extended list of writings by Shakers. The bibliography is thorough, though not annotated.

Churches of Christ/Disciples of Christ

395. McAllister, Lester G., and William E. Tucker. *Journey in Faith: A History of the Christian Church/Disciples of Christ*. St. Louis: Bethany, 1975.
    A comprehensive history of the Stone-Campbell movement. Includes a "Guide to the Literature of the Christian Church (Disciples of Christ)," pp. 464–88.

396. Toulouse, Mark G. *Joined in Discipleship: The Maturing of an American Religious Movement*. St. Louis: Chalice, 1992.
    Thematic essays on key doctrinal issues within the Christian Church/Disciples of Christ tradition.

Christian and Missionary Alliance

397. Ayer, H. D. *The Christian and Missionary Alliance: An Annotated Bibliography of Textual Sources*. Lanham, Md.: Scarecrow, 2001.

An inventory of books, essays, articles, theses, pamphlets, etc., listed by author. A list of periodical sources, and indexes by name and subject, are included.

Brethren Churches

398. *The Brethren Encyclopedia.* 2 vols. Philadelphia: Brethren Encyclopedia, 1983–1984.
The subject of this work is the German Brethren communities (Brethren Church, Church of the Brethren, Dunkard Brethren, etc.). Illustrated. Where they are available, entries include bibliographic citations.

Anabaptist, Mennonite

399. Bender, Harold S., et al., eds. *The Mennonite Encyclopedia: A Comprehensive Reference Work on the Anabaptist-Mennonite Movement.* 5 vols. Hillsboro, Kans.: Mennonite Brethren Pub. House, 1955–1990.
Intended to cover topics, themes, and events from the beginnings of the Anabaptist movement to 1990, drawing in some cases from earlier, European works (e.g., *Mennonitisches Lexikon*, 1913). Especially as a historical source, this set has great value. There are bibliographies with many entries.

400. Hillerbrand, Hans J. *Anabaptist Bibliography, 1520–1630.* Rev. ed. St. Louis: Center for Reformation Research, 1991.
A thorough, topically organized bibliographic source for the serious researcher. Entries are indexed by title and author. The vast bulk of works cited are in German.

401. Swartley, Willard M., and Cornelius J. Dyck. *Annotated Bibliography of Mennonite Writings on War and Peace: 1930–1980.* Scottdale, Pa.: Herald, 1987.
A compendious (700+ pages) work on this central facet of Anabaptist thought. Writings are gathered under topical headings, annotations are carefully written, and the author index provides a helpful means of pulling together writings of key figures (e.g., Sider, Yoder).

402. Williams, George H. *The Radical Reformation.* Philadelphia: Westminster, 1963.
See #175.

The Church in India

403. Menachery, George, ed. *The St. Thomas Christian Encyclopedia of India.* 3 vols. Trichur: St. Thomas Christian Encyclopedia of India, 1982.
Though this work needs revision, it has the merit of having been written about India's Christian tradition by Indian scholars. The diversity and caliber of the articles are impressive, and the maps and illustrations are also extensive.

The Catholic Tradition

General Works

404. *The Official Catholic Directory.* New York: P. J. Kenedy & Sons, 1913–.
The two major sections in this mammoth volume (2,000+ pages) provide exhaustive information on (and contacts for) the administration of the Catholic Church in North America. This includes everything from lists of cardinals to educational institutions from the national to the diocesan and even the parochial level.

405. Day, Peter. *A Dictionary of Religious Orders.* London and New York: Burns and Oates, 2001.
Provides ready access to an otherwise bewildering array of religious orders, communities, etc., in the Western church. Alternate names of orders are clearly denoted. A glossary and a summary list of orders are also useful.

406. Foy, Felician A. *A Concise Guide to the Catholic Church.* Huntington, Ind.: Our Sunday Visitor, 1984.
Here is a basic but serviceable field guide to the contours of the Catholic Church, covering its teaching, liturgy, major historical figures, government, etc. There are few illustrations, and a helpful restraint in the length of entries: serves well as an entry point for the uninitiated. A variety of appendices and a general index are useful in the same way.

Encyclopedias and Dictionaries

407. Carey, Patrick W. *The Roman Catholics.* Westport, Conn.: Greenwood, 1993.
This two-part work includes an overview of American Catholic history and a biographical dictionary of Roman Catholic leaders in America, with a chronology and bibliographic essay.

408. Collinge, William J. *The A to Z of Catholicism.* Lanham, Md., and London: Scarecrow, 2001.
     This quick reference work provides supporting material by way of a chronology (p. 39ff.) and appendices on the popes, ecumenical councils, documents of Vatican II, papal encyclicals, and prayers, a general bibliography, and an index. The dictionary itself runs to almost 500 pages, and the articles are concise but useful, directing the interested reader to further sources.

409. ———. *Historical Dictionary of Catholicism.* Lanham, Md.: Scarecrow, 1997.
     A fine source for quick reference on major ideas, events, and figures within a very broad subject. A chronology (pp. 25–32) and four appendices are helpful features. Bibliography is almost 75 pages.

410. Deedy, John. *The Catholic Fact Book.* Chicago: T. More, 1986.
     A useful one-volume fact book, covering critical information on history, basic beliefs, teachings, institutions, orders, saints, etc.

Papacy

411. Bunson, Matthew. *The Pope Encyclopedia: An A to Z of the Holy See.* New York: Crown Trade Paperbacks, 1995.
     Mostly concise summaries of the popes, their reigns, and other pertinent topics. Appendices include chronology, Roman Curia, and Vatican museums. Includes bibliography.

412. Coppa, Frank J., ed. *Encyclopedia of the Vatican and Papacy.* Westport, Conn.: Greenwood, 1999.
     This volume considers the influence not only of the papacy but of the Vatican, especially since the Renaissance. For its conciseness, breadth, and bibliographies, this is an extremely useful volume.

413. Kelly, J. N. D. *Oxford Dictionary of Popes.* New York: Oxford University Press, 1986.
     Amid the many reference sources on the papacy there is room for a "less is more" approach, and this is as good as any. The author provides good, quick-reference material on the popes, along with short bibliographies. An appendix on Pope Joan and a general index are included.

414. Levillain, Philippe, ed. *The Papacy: An Encyclopedia.* 3 vols. New York and London: Routledge, 2002.
     English translation of an earlier work in French. Consequently, as good as the extensive articles themselves are, few of the considerable biblio-

graphic sources are in English. Volume 3 includes appendices (Chronological List of Popes, Martyred Popes, Popes Who Are Saints) and an index to all three volumes of more than 100 pages.

415. Maxwell-Stuart, P. G. *Chronicle of the Popes.* New York: Thames and Hudson, 1997.
   A richly illustrated survey. The history of the papacy is grouped under five broad headings, and this helps provide a broad outline of the fortunes of the institution during various periods. Time lines, charts, tables, and a bibliography all enhance the text itself.

Saints

416. Attwater, Donald, and John Cumming, eds. *A New Dictionary of Saints.* Collegeville, Minn.: Liturgical Press, 1997.
   Entries are typically no more than a few sentences in length, but the authors succeed in including many saints not mentioned in other reference sources. General dates and feast days are included in entries.

417. ———, eds. *The Penguin Dictionary of Saints.* 3rd ed. London: Penguin, 1995.
   A fine balance of conciseness and utility, combining short but pithy entries on the saints with helpful introductions on the martyrs, the confessors, canonization, etc., and a glossary, reading list, tables on patron saints, emblems, and feast days.

418. Farmer, David Hugh. *The Oxford Dictionary of Saints.* 4th ed. Oxford and New York: Oxford University Press, 1997.
   The entries for this volume are short, yet they contain better bibliographies than some lengthier works. Another feature is the appendices on patronages (example: "Hairdressers [men's]: Martin de Porres, Cosmas and Damian"), emblems, dates, and locations.

419. Guiley, Rosemary Ellen. *The Encyclopedia of Saints.* New York: Facts on File, 2001.
   The choices of reference sources on "saints" is quite extensive, and this newer work has several fine features. First, its articles are generally longer than those offered in other volumes. Second, many of its articles not only offer a list for "Further Reading" but include Web resources within these citations. Third, it contains considerably more (and better) illustrations than most works in its field. Example: the entry on Patrick is about 2½ pages in length, includes a black-and-white illustration, and under "Further Reading" cites Web versions of "The Hymn of Fiacc"

and "The Confession of St. Patrick." The concise general bibliography at the conclusion of the work also includes four Websites.

420. Jones, Kathleen. *A Basic Dictionary of Saints.* Norwich, UK: Canterbury, 2001.
The function of this work (only 131 pages long) is to provide quick-reference information. Illustrations are few. It does include a time line, a glossary, and short list for further reading.

421. *The Book of Saints: A Dictionary of Servants of God.* 6th ed. Wilton, Conn.: Morehouse, 1994.
A unique feature of this work is its having been originally compiled in 1921 by Benedictine monks in an English abbey. Entries are short, feast days are included, as are a list of emblems, a short bibliography, and some illustrations.

422. Walsh, Michael, ed. *Butler's Lives of Patron Saints.* San Francisco: Harper & Row, 1989.
This is a fairly recent abridgment of an older four-volume work (1756–1759). Because this work goes beyond basic biographical information to provide some of the "narratives of beatification," it serves a broader and different purpose than other dictionaries of saints. There are indexes of dates and persons.

Theology

423. Downey, Michael, ed. *The New Dictionary of Catholic Spirituality.* Collegeville, Minn.: Liturgical Press, 1993.
Intended to serve as a companion to *New Dictionary of Theology* and the *New Dictionary of Sacramental Worship* (see ##221, 470), this volume surveys the landscape of spirituality in a post–Vatican II setting. Topical index provides an additional point of entry to a field that tends to be unwieldy.

424. Dulles, Avery, and Patrick Granfield. *The Church: A Bibliography.* Wilmington, Del.: Glazier, 1985.
A topical bibliography of literature about the church as understood through history, by two distinguished Roman Catholic theologians.

425. ———. *The Theology of the Church: A Bibliography.* New York: Paulist, 2000.
An extensive revision of #424, adding over 600 new items and deleting some others. An essential point of reference for any student, within any Christian community, who wants to explore this subject. Entries

are arranged under a wide variety of headings, and a name index is included.

426. Dwyer, Judith A., ed. *The New Dictionary of Catholic Social Thought.* Collegeville, Minn.: Liturgical Press, 1994.
The purpose of this volume is to present a post–Vatican II treatment of recent social encyclicals, as well as a Catholic consideration of various moral issues. (Example: the essay on "Human Rights" is 15 pages in length, with a bibliography of moderate length.) The indexes and cross-references are extensive.

427. Komonchak, Joseph A., et al., eds. *The New Dictionary of Theology.* Wilmington, Del.: Glazier, 1987.
See #221.

428. Shaw, Russell, ed. *Our Sunday Visitor's Encyclopedia of Catholic Doctrine.* Huntington, Ind.: Our Sunday Visitor Pub., 1997.
See #239.

Dictionaries and Encyclopedias

429. Glazier, Michael, and Monika K. Hellwig, eds. *The Modern Catholic Encyclopedia.* Collegeville, Minn.: Liturgical Press, 1994.
See #233.

430. Hardon, John A. *Modern Catholic Dictionary.* Garden City, N.Y.: Doubleday, 1980.
See #234.

431. McBrien, Richard P., ed. *The HarperCollins Encyclopedia of Catholicism.* New York: HarperCollins, 1995.
See #235.

432. Stravinskas, Peter M. J., ed. *Our Sunday Visitor's Catholic Encyclopedia.* Huntingon, Ind.: Our Sunday Visitor Pub., 1998.
This work presents itself to the more general reader, who wants a brief overview. The entries themselves are generally concise, in some cases including illustrations. No bibliographies are included.

History

433. Ellis, John Tracy. *A Guide to American Catholic History.* Santa Barbara: ABC-Clio, 1982.

A dated but thorough annotated bibliographic guide to the literature. Subheadings on diocesan and parish history, biographies and correspondence, religious communities, etc., are included, as is a general index.

434. Glazier, Michael, and Thomas J. Shelley, eds. *The Encyclopedia of American Catholic History*. Collegeville, Minn.: Liturgical Press, 1997.
See #182.

Documents and Tradition

435. Abbot, Walter M., ed. *The Documents of Vatican II: In a New and Definitive Translation, with Commentaries and Notes by Catholic, Protestant, and Orthodox Authorities*. New York: Crossroad, 1989.
Puts all the documents in a very helpful setting. Each section is accompanied by an introduction and a response by various scholars and clerics. Very well indexed.

436. *Catechism of the Catholic Church*. Vatican City: Libreri Editrice Vaticana, 2000.
The most recent English edition of the basic teachings of the Catholic Church, including an exposition of the creeds, the sacraments, the Ten Commandments, prayer, etc. Indexes, glossary, and some color illustrations are provided.

437. Flannery, Austin, ed. *Documents of Vatican II*, and *Vatican Council II: More Postconciliar Documents*. Grand Rapids: Eerdmans, 1984.
These works provide a convenient edition of the text of the documents, along with extensive commentaries, a descriptive catalog, and a general index.

438. Tanner, Norman P., ed. *Decrees of the Ecumenical Councils*. 2 vols. Washington, D.C.: Georgetown University Press, 1990.
"Contains the original text with a facing English translation of all the twenty-one councils (Nicaea I in 325 to Vatican II in 1962" (p. vii). Volume 2 includes indexes by chronology, scriptural reference, names, etc.

Renewal Movements

439. Bord, Richard J., and Joseph E. Faulkner. *The Catholic Charismatics: The Anatomy of a Modern Religious Movement*. University Park, Pa., and London: Pennsylvania State University Press, 1984.

Two scholars analyze the roots, energy, structure, theology, and social consciousness of this renewal movement.

440. Byrne, James E. *Living in the Spirit: A Handbook on Catholic Charismatic Christianity.* New York: Paulist Press, 1975.

An early description and outline of what has become one of the fastest-growing sectors of the Catholic Church, especially in Latin America.

The Eastern Orthodox Tradition

441. Atiya, Aziz S., ed. *The Coptic Encyclopedia.* 3 vols. New York: Maxwell Macmillan International, 1991.

A thorough survey of all subjects relating to the history, archaeology, learning, writings, etc., within the Coptic Christian tradition. There is a good general bibliography early in vol. 1, and each article has its own bibliography as well.

442. Day, Peter D. *The Liturgical Dictionary of Eastern Christianity.* Collegeville, Md.: Liturgical Press, 1993.

See #240.

443. Demetrakopoulos, George H. *Dictionary of Orthodox Theology: A Summary of the Beliefs, Practices and History of the Eastern Orthodox Church.* New York: Philosophical Library, 1964.

See #241.

444. Frazer, Ruth F., ed. *Eastern Christianity: A Bibliography Selected from the ATLA Religion Database.* Chicago: American Theological Library Association, 1984.

Lengthy list of citations produced from the electronic version of the ATLA Religion Database.

445. Litsas, Fotios K., ed. *A Companion to the Greek Orthodox Church: Essays and References.* New York: Department of Communication, Greek Orthodox Archdiocese of North and South America, 1984.

See #242.

446. Ormanian, Malachia. *A Dictionary of the Armenian Church.* Trans. Bedros Norehad. New York: St. Vartan Press, 1984.

An English translation of a 1905 Armenian work. Short entries under the headings of Feasts, Vessels and Vestments, and Nocturn.

447. Parry, Ken, et al., eds. *The Blackwell Dictionary of Eastern Christianity.* Oxford, UK; Malden, Mass.: Blackwell, 1999.
    See #243.

448. Patrinacos, Nicon D. *A Dictionary of Greek Orthodoxy.* Pleasantville, N.Y.: Hellenic Heritage Pub., 1984.
    See #244.

449. Prokurat, Michael, et al. *Historical Dictionary of the Orthodox Church.* Lanham, Md.: Scarecrow, 1996.
    See #245.

Other Traditions

Mormonism

450. Allen, James B., et al., eds. *Studies in Mormon History, 1830–1997: An Indexed Bibliography.* Urbana, Ill.: University of Illinois Press, 2000.
    Daunting in size except to the most ambitious scholar, this work of 1,000+ pages cites more than 2,600 books, more than 10,400 articles, more than 1,800 theses and dissertations, etc. (This work represents a model of thoroughness and determination as a print-based bibliography.)

451. Bitton, Davis. *Historical Dictionary of Mormonism.* 2nd ed. Metuchen, N.J.: Scarecrow, 2000.
    Entries of moderate length on the central facts, events, and persons in the Mormon tradition. The dictionary is enhanced by the inclusion of a chronology, extended bibliography, and appendices of various kinds.

452. Eborn, Bret A. *Comprehensive Bibliography of Mormon Literature.* Peoria, Az.: Eborn, 1997.
    The literature of Mormonism is both extensive and diverse, and this work represents an attempt to bring order to things from the vantage point of a book dealer. Attempts to provide an extensive, though not comprehensive, listing of books relating to Mormonism. No annotations.

453. Shields, Steven L. *The Latter Day Saint Churches: An Annotated Bibliography.* New York and London: Garland, 1987.
    This work's special contribution is to draw attention to the surprising range of splinter and dissident movements loosely associated with Mormonism in history. For this complex but doctrinally unwieldy subject, a work like this is absolutely necessary.

Jehovah's Witnesses

454. Bergman, Jerry, ed. *Jehovah's Witnesses: A Comprehensive and Selectively Annotated Bibliography.* Westport, Conn.: Greenwood, 1999.

The ideal starting point for any researcher interested in scholarly study of the Jehovah's Witnesses. The introduction gives a historical summary of the genesis and development of this movement, and the editor's introductory notes to each of the sections are also helpful.

The Religious Right

455. Utter, Glenn H., and John W. Storey. *The Religious Right: A Reference Handbook.* 2nd ed. Santa Barbara and Oxford: ABC-Clio, 2001.

A profile of a specific religious group, using surveys and data gathering. Covers survey of attitudes, organizations, print and media resources.

Chapter 8

Practical Theology

There is far less substantive reference material available in practical theology than in any of the other traditional areas of seminary education (Bible, history, theology). But it is likely that this does not indicate a lack of scholarly activity so much as that by its very nature praxis is much harder to codify, to put between the covers of a book in some kind of definitive form. It may also be true that proportionally more scholarly interchange in this field occurs through professional journals, conferences and seminars, etc.

Whatever the explanation for the shortage, it is fortunate that amid the available resources are some excellent works, particularly newer publications on worship and education. Works cited here are grouped under the familiar headings of:

Pastoral Care and Counseling
Religious Education
Preaching
Worship and Music

Pastoral Care and Counseling

Bibliography

456. Gorman, G. E., and Lyn Gorman. *Theological and Religious Reference Materials.* Vol. 3: *Practical Theology.* Westport, Conn.: Greenwood, 1986.

Thorough annotations make this a rich source of bibliographic information. Separate sections are included on Practical Theology generally, Liturgy and Worship, Homiletics, Education, Counseling, and Sociology. There are indexes by author, title, and subject.

Dictionaries and Encyclopedias

457. Campbell, Alastair V., ed. *A Dictionary of Pastoral Care*. London: SPCK, 1987.
    In the space of only about 300 pages this work's 300 entries provide careful coverage of the key themes and concepts in the field. (Example: the entry on "Pastoral Theology" is two pages long, is accompanied by eight bibliographic sources, and is cross-referenced to three other entries.)

458. Carr, Wesley, ed. *The New Dictionary of Pastoral Studies*. Grand Rapids: Eerdmans, 2002.
    Incorporating more than 700 entries by 200 contributors, this volume is a welcome update to the reference literature in the field, going a long way toward bringing treatment of the subject up to date. There is a thorough general bibliography at the end. Placing bibliographies with the articles themselves would have made this work even better.

459. Hunter, Rodney J., ed. *Dictionary of Pastoral Care and Counseling*. Nashville: Abingdon, 1990.
    The breadth and depth of this work (1,300+ pages) qualifies it as an encyclopedia, rather than a dictionary. This work's objectives are to provide practical information, to integrate practice with theological and social theory, to provide focus and identity for pastoral care, and to promote ecumenical consciousness and understanding (pp. xi–xii). Bibliographies and cross references are extensive.

Religious Education

460. Anthony, Michael J., ed. *Evangelical Dictionary of Christian Education*. Grand Rapids: Baker, 2001.
    This comprehensive resource is the work of a sizable contingent of evangelical scholars in the field. The bibliographies are not distributed consistently (some longer articles include them, others do not). The outlook of the work (if it is possible to generalize with a work this large) is that of the church rather than the academy: an emphasis on specifically *Christian* rather than broadly *religious* education.

461. Atkinson, Harley, ed. *Handbook of Young Adult Religious Education*. Birmingham, Ala.: Religious Education Press, 1995.

As the name implies, this work presents a collection of topical essays. These are contributed by a variety of authors under five general headings: Foundations of Young Adult Religious Education, Characteristics of Young Adults, Educational Procedures, Focused Religious Education for Young Adults, and Programming Young Adult Religious Education. Tables and illustrations are included. Good bibliographies accompany the individual chapters.

462. Cully, Iris V., and Kendig Brubaker Cully, eds. *Harper's Encyclopedia of Religious Education*. San Francisco: Harper & Row, 1990.
The combination of short entries and longer essays (e.g., "Child Development"), with limited illustrations and bibliographies, makes this a good reference tool for a field that often resists clear definition. Articles vary from topics to persons to concepts, doctrines, etc.

463. Devitt, Patrick M. *That You May Believe: A Brief History of Religious Education*. Dublin: Dominican Publications, 1992.
This brief work (125 pp.) covers a remarkable amount of material outlining the topic within the Catholic tradition, from earliest times to the twentieth century. Notes and bibliography are extensive.

464. Towns, Elmer L. *Towns' Sunday School Encyclopedia*. Wheaton, Ill.: Tyndale, 1993.
Though this work is an encyclopedia of the author's own thoughts, observations, and extensive experience in this area, it still draws together broadly useful insights on a church institution that has recently been in decline.

465. Wyckoff, D. Campbell, and George Brown, eds. *Religious Education, 1960–1993: An Annotated Bibliography*. Westport, Conn.: Greenwood, 1995.
Along with some introductory essays ("Foundations of Religious Education," "Religious Education Theory," "Religion and Higher Education," etc.) this work annotates more than 1,100 published items in the field. Needs to be updated, but remains an essential resource for surveying the scholarship during its prescribed time period. Includes name and title indexes.

Preaching

466. Duduit, Michael, ed. *Handbook of Contemporary Preaching*. Nashville: Broadman, 1992.
An anthology of recent thought on preaching, from a wide range of about fifty contributors. There are extensive notes with each chapter, and a general bibliography at the conclusion.

467. Gugliotto, Lee J. *Handbook for Bible Study: A Guide to Understanding, Teaching, and Preaching the Word of God.* Hagerstown, Md.: Review and Herald, 1995.
    See #58.

468. Willimon, William H., and Richard Lischer, eds. *Concise Encyclopedia of Preaching.* Louisville: Westminster John Knox Press, 1995.
    More a dictionary than an encyclopedia, this resource provides useful quick reference for broad reflections or specific information on preaching. Entries range from brief references to longer essays, most with bibliographies. (Example: the entry on "Homiletics and Preaching in Latin America," 2½ pages in length, contains a historical overview, identification of key figures, and reference to denominations and training.)

Worship and Music

469. Davies, J. G., ed. *The New Westminster Dictionary of Liturgy and Worship.* Philadelphia: Westminster, 1986.
    Though a revision is overdue, this may still be the best ready-reference work on the subject, covering a rich expanse of traditions and subjects with interest and care.

470. Fink, Peter E., ed. *The New Dictionary of Sacramental Worship.* Collegeville, Minn.: Liturgical Press, 1990.
    This expansive Catholic work was written a generation after Vatican II and provides a thorough guide to tradition, thought, and practice in Catholic worship. There are some limitations to its structure: the lack of a good introductory essay (or essays) and a too-brief table of contents create an imbalance between the amount of material and the possible points of access to that material.

471. Foley, Edward, ed. *Worship Music: A Concise Dictionary.* Collegeville, Minn.: Liturgical Press, 2000.
    This Catholic quick-reference source emphasizes the terminology and tradition of worship music in North America. All of the articles are concise, and only the longer of these (e.g., "Chorale") include a bibliography. (Example: the entry on "Fauré, Gabriel," consists of one long paragraph, providing dates, notes on his career, and sample titles of his compositions.)

472. Hatchett, Marion J. *A Guide to the Practice of Church Music.* New York: Church Hymnal Corp., 1991.

This work serves several functions: it provides a primer on the role of music in the life of a church, a bibliographic guide, and a structured guide to integrating music with other elements of services for various occasions. Its chapters map out the musical ministries typical of a church, list hymns (and procedures for their evaluation and selection), address the challenge of educating the congregation in church music, and provide counsel on careful planning of services for various occasions. Three appendices provide information on alternate musical arrangements, a metrical index of tunes from the 1982 Episcopal Hymnal, and (at some length) present check lists for planning a wide variety of services. Though compiled within an Episcopal ethos, this work has many resources of value to clergy and musicians in churches of every kind.

473. Lang, Jovian. *Dictionary of the Liturgy.* New York: Catholic Book Pub., 1989.

On a smaller and more approachable level, this work has similar aims to #470. An especially useful guide for those who are either outsiders or newcomers to worship in the Roman Catholic tradition.

474. Music, David W. *Christian Hymnody in Twentieth-Century Britain and America: An Annotated Bibliography.* Westport, Conn., and London: Greenwood, 2001.

A major contribution of this work is to take inventory of the subject during a period of great musical and cultural change, inside and outside the church. The five chapters arrange citations under the headings of a Historical Overview, Repertory, Language, Practice, and People. A general index is included.

475. Perry, Michael. *Preparing for Worship: The Essential Handbook for Worship Leaders.* London: Marshall Pickering, 1995.

An eminently useful guide for those who lead worship. Provides thoughtful reflections on worship, as well as a wealth of direction on everything from copyright issues to indexes of hymns' first lines.

476. Pfatteicher, Philip H. *A Dictionary of Liturgical Terms.* Philadelphia: Trinity Press International, 1991.

This quick-reference tool provides a concise glossary (and pronunciation guide) of words used in talking about liturgy and worship. Words from French (*Prie Dieu*), Greek (*Kyrie Pantokrator*), and Latin (*Gaudete*) as well as English are included. There is no index or bibliography.

477. Poultney, David. *Dictionary of Western Church Music.* Chicago and London: American Library Association, 1991.

A quick-reference source such as this one can serve a useful role in providing simple and accessible information on the vocabulary of church music. Most of the entries describe terms, genres, and composers in the field. There are several appendices, which provide data on publishers, societies and organizations, and periodicals.

478. Skoglund, John E. *A Manual of Worship*. New ed. Valley Forge, Pa.: Judson, 1993.
This book serves as a guide to "free church" worship, i.e., settings that do not have prescribed forms. Selections provide frameworks for various worship settings, as well as examples of prayers for specific occasions. For nonliturgical contexts, this manual provides excellent structures and guidelines for strengthening worship practices. A glossary is included.

479. Stake, Donald Wilson. *The ABCs of Worship: A Concise Dictionary*. Louisville: Westminster/John Knox, 1992.
This work serves as a field guide to worship terms and practices, for the many who want to learn more. Definitions are mostly brief, and written in nontechnical language. There are numerous cross-references, as well as suggestions for further reading.

480. Routley, Eric. *An English-Speaking Hymnal Guide*. Collegeville, Minn.: Liturgical Press, 1979.
Though dated, this work by an eminent hymnologist examines different hymnals in English and presents helpful guidelines for evaluation. The opening section of the work outlines the kinds of sources on hymnody that are available, and the longest section of the book itemizes hymns and identifies hymnals in which those selections appear. An index of authors and a brief bibliography are included.

481. Spencer, Donald A. *Hymn and Scripture Selection Guide: A Cross-Reference Tool for Worship Leaders*. Revised and expanded. Grand Rapids: Baker, 1993.
This work presents an innovative approach to matching hymns with other elements of the service, arranging hymns according to Scripture references, topics, etc. The guide is arranged in four sections: Hymns with Scripture References, Scripture with Hymn References, Topical Index, and finally an Index of Hymns.

482. Thompson, Bard, ed. *A Bibliography of Christian Worship*. Philadelphia: American Theological Library Association; Metuchen, N.J.: Scarecrow, 1989.
At almost 800 pages this bibliographic resource provides an excellent inventory of what had been written about worship up to its date of publication.

483. Von Ende, Richard Chaffey. *Church Music: An International Bibliography.*
Metuchen, N.J., and London: Scarecrow, 1980.
This book's almost 6,000 unannotated entries are grouped under some
284 categories, including denominations, hymnals and songbooks,
national and/or geographic entities, etc.

484. Webber, Robert E., ed. *The Complete Library of Christian Worship.* 7 vols.
Nashville: Star Song Pub., 1993.
The stated purpose of this work is "to make biblical, historical, and
contemporary resources on worship available to pastors, music ministers, worship committees, and the motivated individual worshiper."
The entire work combines a biblical, theological, and historical framework with resources for worship-in-practice. Thus it functions as a
hybrid of encyclopedia, historical dictionary, and a work of practical
theology. The indexes and bibliographies are extensive.

485. White, James F. *Documents of Christian Worship: Descriptive and Interpretive
Sources.* Louisville: Westminster/John Knox, 1992.
This helpful sourcebook comprises an excellent anthology of thought
and writings on Christian worship, for those who want to better understand worship traditions. The work is divided into chapters under the
headings of various dimensions of worship (teaching, prayer, sacraments, etc.). It is very useful to have the excerpts from a historical range
of Christian writers on matters relating to worship. This source also
includes good bibliographies and indexes.

Chapter 9

Christian Spirituality

The addition of a brief chapter on this subject may seem unusual, though it ought not to be so. The intention is not to treat Christian spirituality as a subject comparable to, say, church history or archaeology, but rather to serve a balancing function to a mainly academic emphasis in many seminaries, as well as to remind ourselves that the study of theology and the practice of ministry are essentially spiritual pursuits. Especially in the seminary setting there is often a deep-seated fear of piety (or even the appearance of piety), and occasionally this is a legitimate response to an oversubjectifying of the Christian faith. But there are sometimes at least equal (though less easy to express) grounds for concern about the loss of the sense of the spiritual in the midst of this kind of study and reflection.

Of course, the difficulty about even offering a few suggestions is that spirituality is so fundamentally *personal*—"when you pray, go into your closet and shut the door" were the directions Jesus gave—and it is a little awkward commending books for such a setting. But (1) it would seem to me more of an oversight *not* to recognize this dimension of the life of theological study than to recognize it; (2) an effort has been made in these brief recommendations to include some works that have endured, and so can at least be consulted with some assurance that they have been of benefit to other readers.

The following works are grouped under:

General Works
Books on Prayer
Anthologies

General Works

486. Allen, Diogenes. *Spiritual Theology: The Theology of Yesterday for Spiritual Help Today*. Cambridge· Cowley, 1997.
    An overview by a philosopher and theologian on the nature, contours, and practices of spiritual theology. Offers a basic and helpful introduction to a subject that has not been well defined or much attended to (at least within Protestantism) in recent times. Each chapter provides endnotes, and there is a general index at the end.

487. Jones, Cheslyn, et al., eds. *The Study of Spirituality*. New York: Oxford University Press, 1986.
    Draws on the expertise of more than sixty writers to cover the theology of spirituality, the history of spirituality, and pastoral spirituality (with greatest emphasis on the second). Remarkably diverse in its interests, treating both essential and lesser-known figures and traditions. Includes bibliographies and indexes.

488. Wakefield, Gordon S., ed. *The Westminster Dictionary of Christian Spirituality*. Philadelphia: Westminster, 1986.
    See #21.

Books on Prayer

489. Appleton, George, ed. *The Oxford Book of Prayer.* New York and Oxford: Oxford University Press, 1985.
    Selections are grouped as follows: "Prayers from the Scriptures," "Prayers of the Church," "Prayer as Listening," "Prayers from Other Traditions," "Prayers for the Unity of Mankind." Indexes of authors and sources are included.

490. Chariton, Igumen. *The Art of Prayer: An Orthodox Anthology*. London: Faber and Faber, 1997.
    This collection was compiled by a Russian Orthodox monk during the first half of the twentieth century. An introduction of 40 pages puts the subject in historical and cultural context. Teachings and examples of

prayer are included in six chapters, which are followed by a list for further reading and an index.

491. Church, F. Forrester, and Terrence J. Mulry, eds. *The Macmillan Book of Earliest Christian Prayers.* New York: Macmillan, 1988.
Selections are included from the New Testament period up to Augustine of Hippo. Each of the fifteen subsections is given a brief introduction. A devotional-topical and a source-name index are provided.

492. Collins, Owen, ed. *2000 Years of Classic Christian Prayers: A Collection for Public and Personal Use.* Maryknoll, N.Y.: Orbis, 2000.
In addition to a rich selection of prayers under a variety of headings, this work provides indexes by first line, by subject, by authors and sources, and by biblical reference, but does not provide bibliographic resources.

493. Counsell, Michael, ed. *2000 Years of Prayer.* Harrisburg: Morehouse, 1999.
It is hard to imagine any anthology incorporating more prayers, under such a variety of themes and subheadings, than this one does in about 650 pages. These categories reflect the historical, thematic, and geographical richness represented by the prayers of the church and its people. An index of themes and first lines, and a thorough listing of notes and acknowledgments, facilitate further study.

494. Davies, Horton, ed. *The Communion of Saints: Prayers of the Famous.* Grand Rapids: Eerdmans, 1990.
Arranges prayers under broad headings ("Intercession," "The Christian Year," etc.). It is the people whose prayers are cited that make this anthology unique (authors, statesmen, artists, etc., whose careers and accomplishments we would not usually associate with a life of prayer). As such, these prayers tend to reflect uncommon perspectives, and to arise from different life circumstances than is the case with those found in other anthologies. There is a general index and a bibliography.

495. Kiley, Mark, ed. *Prayer from Alexander to Constantine: A Critical Anthology.* London and New York: Routledge, 1997.
Fifty prayer texts covering 650 years, from Jewish, Christian, and pagan (Greek and Roman) religions. Each individual selection is introduced by a scholar in the respective field, and is provided with notes and a useful bibliography. A glossary and general index are included.

496. Van de Weyer, Robert, ed. *The HarperCollins Book of Prayer: A Treasury of Prayer Through the Ages.* San Francisco: HarperSanFrancisco, 1993.
See #20.

Anthologies

497. Adels, Jill Haak, ed. *The Wisdom of the Saints: An Anthology.* New York: Oxford University Press, 1987.
    Selections from the writings of saints (both "official" and "unofficial") from the earliest times to the present, arranged thematically ("God," "Sacrifice," "Virtue," etc.). This arrangement accommodates fewer saints, but lets them speak at greater length than other works. Biographical sketches on each saint are included at the conclusion (pp. 205–33). Because this work lacks an index, it serves best as a source for quick reference and quotations.

498. Atwell, Robert, ed. *Spiritual Classics from the Early Church: Anthology.* London: National Society/Church House Pub., 1995.
    The literature of Christian spirituality is so vast, and its self-definition at times so vague, that a basic introduction to the major figures and themes such as this one can be very useful. There are eight chapters (Cyprian, Desert Tradition, Basil the Great, Gregory of Nyssa, John Chrysostom, Augustine, Benedict, and Gregory the Great). Each chapter includes a historical introduction, excerpts from the subject at hand, notes, and select bibliography. A general bibliography and index are also included.

499. Blackburn, E. A., et al., eds. *A Treasury of the Kingdom: An Anthology.* New York and London: Oxford University Press, 1954.
    Under five general headings (Approach to the Kingdom, Festivals of the Kingdom, Fruit of the Kingdom, Servants of the Kingdom, Kingdom Perfected), readings illustrative of the spiritual quest are helpfully introduced and arranged.

500. Cousins, Ewert, ed. *World Spirituality: An Encyclopedic History of the Religious Quest.* New York: Crossroad, 1985–.
    This encyclopedic series is projected to include 25 volumes, surveying the spiritual traditions of several of the great religions. Of particular interest for the present work are vols. 16 (*Christian Spirituality: Origins to the Twelfth Century*), 17 (*Christian Spirituality: High Middle Ages and Reformation*), and 18 (*Christian Spirituality: Post-Reformation and Modern.* Each volume is the work of many contributors, and excellent bibliographies are included.

501. De Bertodano, Teresa, ed. *Treasury of the Catholic Church: Two Thousand Years of Spiritual Writing.* London: Darton, Longman, and Todd, 1999.
    Like #497, this volume arranges selections thematically, though in this case the headings are fewer and more broad ("Love," "Creation and

Redemption," "Growing and Serving," etc.). Bibliographic sources for the selections are listed at the conclusion of the book, as are notes and brief historical data on the authors.

502. Dupré, Louis, and James A. Wiseman. *Light from Light: An Anthology of Christian Mysticism.* 2nd ed. New York and Mahwah, N.J.: Paulist Press, 2001.
Twenty-one selections from Origen to Thomas Merton, each with its own introduction and bibliography. Example: the entry on "Catherine of Siena" is 18 pages, including 3 pages of historical and biographical background, followed by 13 pages of excerpts from two of her works. A page of bibliography is included for this entry.

503. Egan, Harvey, ed. *An Anthology of Christian Mysticism.* Collegeville, Minn.: Liturgical Press, 1991.
An introductory chapter outlines biblical mysticism, and this is followed by selections from Origen to Karl Rahner. Each has its own biographical sketch. There are a selected bibliography, extensive endnotes, and an index of authors and titles.

504. Fleming, David, ed. *The Fire and the Cloud: An Anthology of Catholic Spirituality.* New York: Paulist Press, 1978.
Concentrates on key figures and movements in the development of the Catholic spiritual tradition, beginning with Ignatius of Antioch and extending to Thomas Merton. Bibliographical sources are scanty: this work is best considered an introductory reader.

505. Joyce, Timothy. *Celtic Christianity: A Sacred Tradition, a Vision of Hope.* Maryknoll, N.Y.: Orbis, 1998.
A good practical introduction to a pre-Reformation still in process of being rediscovered by Protestant Christianity. Provides an overview of the differences between Celtic and modern Christianity, the history and development of Celtic monasticism, and the decline of Celtic traditions. Includes notes, bibliography, and index.

506. McGuckin, John. *At the Lighting of the Lamps: Hymns of the Ancient Church.* Harrisburg: Morehouse, 1995.
The distinctive purpose of this book is to present 31 hymn texts from the early church, both in the original Greek or Latin and in English translation, and brief notes on the origins and settings of each. A brief select bibliography is included.

507. Madigan, Shawn, ed. *Mystics, Visionaries, and Prophets: A Historical Anthology of Women's Spiritual Writings.* Minneapolis: Fortress, 1998.

"This anthology seeks to gather the religious wisdom, social vision, and personal insight of Christian women over twenty centuries" (p. 3). This work represents an attempt to fill a regrettable gap in reference literature: collections of spiritual writings by women. The biographical/historical introductions to the various writers are clear and thorough, bibliographies are thorough, and there is a general index.

508. Magill, Frank N., and Ian P. McGreal. *Christian Spirituality: The Essential Guide to the Most Influential Spiritual Writings of the Christian Tradition.* New York: Harper & Row, 1988.
See #19.

509. Mandelker, Amy, and Elizabeth Powers, eds. *Pilgrim Souls: An Anthology of Spiritual Autobiographies.* New York: Simon & Schuster, 1999.
Entries are grouped under four headings: Wanderers and Seekers, Pilgrims and Missionaries, Mystics and Visionaries, and Philosophers and Scholars. Various religious traditions are represented. Each "pilgrim" is given a brief introduction, and several examples of his/her work are included. Example: the entry on Albert Schweitzer includes a page of biographical background and about three pages of excerpts from his *Out of My Life and Thought.*

510. Tyson, John R., ed. *Invitation to Christian Spirituality: An Ecumenical Anthology.* New York: Oxford University Press, 1999.
An extended introductory essay (pp. 1–52) outlines what is meant by "Christian Spirituality." Excerpts of Christian writers from Ignatius of Antioch to Archbishop Desmond Tutu are included under five historical headings. Each selection includes a brief introduction; bibliographic sources are listed in footnotes. A general and a scriptural index are provided.

511. Van de Weyer, Robert, ed. *Roots of Faith: An Anthology of Early Christian Spirituality to Contemplate and Treasure.* Grand Rapids: Eerdmans, 1997.
Brief selections from the early church, from Clement of Rome through Tertullian. Includes color plates and an introductory essay that concludes: "the Early Fathers are not read nearly as widely as they deserve; this book is an attempt to put that right" (p. 9). Each author is given a brief introduction. Includes index.

Chapter 10

Christianity and Literature

This final chapter found a place in this revision for several reasons. First, the entire book is devoted to surveying the *literature*, not merely the facts, the concepts, or the "data" of theology. This discipline has its own history, its own vocabulary, and its own modes of expression, ranging from notes, to lectures, to essays, to dissertations, to sermons. A second reason stems from the first: because all of us carry out most of these activities on personal computers, we are doing far more of our own writing and composition now than was the case a decade or more ago, when one relied on secretaries or typing services. Lastly, the affinities between what writers do and what preachers in particular do seem more evident (and intriguing) all the time, and (given that all of us as students, pastors, etc., spend so much of our time writing) it makes a lot of sense to reflect on theology as a literary endeavor.

This brief selection of titles will be arranged as follows:

Reference Works
Anthologies and Readers
Essays, Lectures, and Studies

Reference Works

512. Ackerman, James S., and Thayer S. Warshaw, eds. *The Bible As/In Literature*. 2nd ed. Glenview, Ill.: Scott Foresman, 1995.

The twofold purpose of this work is to study the literary craftsmanship of passages in the Bible and to explore the relationship of a variety of other stories, poems, and plays to the Bible. Because it provides questions for thought and discussion throughout, the work may be used as (but need not be restricted to) a text for courses. Appendices include a brief history of the Bible, a time line of Bible events, maps, sampling of Bible translations, and a handbook of Bible stories and biblical translations.

513. Jeffrey, David Lyle, ed. *A Dictionary of Biblical Tradition in English Literature*. Grand Rapids: Eerdmans, 1992.

This work represents the collaborative efforts of more than 200 scholars on the relationship between the Bible and the English literary tradition. Entries describe how a word or phrase was used in the Bible, how it was understood in exegetical traditions, and the part it has played in literature. Longer articles include bibliographies. Appendices include extensive bibliographies on biblical studies, history of biblical interpretation, and biblical traditions in English literature.

514. Kari, Daven Michael. *A Bibliography of Sources in Christianity and the Arts*. Lewiston, N.Y.: Edwin Mellen, 1997.

This wide-ranging work includes a section of bibliography on Christianity and literature (pp. 225–300). Topics include literature, literary theory, literary criticism, etc. This work's usefulness would be increased further if annotations are included in an eventual revised edition.

Anthologies and Readers

515. Hayward, S., and S. Lefanu. *God: An Anthology of Fiction*. London and New York: Serpent's Tail, 1992.

An intriguing selection of short stories on religious themes, mostly by lesser-known contemporary authors. Biographical notes on contributors are included at the end.

516. Ingrams, Richard, ed. *Jesus: Authors Take Sides: An Anthology*. London: HarperCollins, 1999.

This book has at least two exceptional virtues: first, it creatively draws together the divergent opinions of writers over time on who Jesus was and what he meant; second, its own inquiring spirit and engaging style provide a fine example of why the literary quest to understand Jesus shows no sign of losing interest. A selection of sources for further reading is included.

517. Jasper, David, and Stephen Prickett, eds. *The Bible and Literature: A Reader.* Oxford, UK, and Malden, Mass.: Blackwell, 1999.

An introduction to the study of the Bible and literature. The unusual plan of this work is to gather excerpts from English literature that allude to or are associated with specific Bible stories or themes (e.g., Jacob and Esau, the prodigal son, etc.). This anthology is made even more useful by the introductory essays contributed by the editors, providing first a historical survey of how the Bible and literature have interacted, and second an outline of current trends in literary readings of the Bible. A general bibliography and name index are included.

518. Larsen, David L. *The Company of the Creative: A Christian Reader's Guide to Great Literature and Its Themes.* Grand Rapids: Kregel, 2001.

This anthology, compiled by a former pastor and professor of homiletics, provides an expansive introduction and survey to English literature from the standpoint of a lover, rather than a critic or theorist, of English literature. There are chapters on classical literature, Shakespeare, poetry (British and American), drama, essays, biography, etc. Subject, title, and author indexes are especially helpful in a work that encompasses so many of each. In addition to copious footnotes, a good general bibliography is provided (as well as a chronology) at the end.

519. McGrath, Alister, ed. *Christian Literature: An Anthology.* Oxford, UK, and Malden, Mass.: Blackwell, 2001.

See #22.

520. Winter, David, ed. *The Poets' Christ: An Anthology of Poetry about Jesus.* Oxford: Lion, 2000.

A brief anthology of poems is presented here grouped under thematic headings (Birth, Teacher and Healer, etc.). This work provides a good sampling of contemporary poetry on Christian themes. Indexes of authors and first lines are included.

Essays, Lectures, and Studies

521. Brown, W. Dale. *Of Fiction and Faith: Twelve American Writers Talk about Their Vision and Work.* Grand Rapids: Eerdmans, 1997.

A fine starting point for anyone wanting to know how specific authors have integrated their spiritual and literary vocations. The author has visited and insightfully interviewed twelve authors including Frederick Buechner, Garrison Keillor, and Will Campbell.

522. Buechner, Frederick. *The Clown in the Belfry: Writings on Faith and Fiction.* San Francisco: HarperSanFrancisco, 1992.

Fourteen reflections and sermons on faith, literature, and writing by a distinguished writer and preacher. These pieces were written for a variety of settings—churches, literary societies, school convocations—and this provides a range of perspectives that is very helpful.

523. Daiches, David. *God and the Poets*. Oxford: Clarendon, 1984.
This book presents Gifford Lectures for 1983 by a literary critic and historian. The main theme of his remarks is natural theology. There are chapters on the book of Job, *Paradise Lost*, on Calvinism from Robert Burns to James Hogg, etc.

524. Davies, Horton. *A Mirror of the Ministry in Modern Novels*. New York: Oxford University Press, 1959.
Though it would be helpful to see a work like this updated, there is still great value in having in one volume both a consideration of the portrayal of clergy in specific settings by individual authors *and* a comprehensive appraisal in the concluding chapter. Most of the best-known examples—Nathaniel Hawthorne, Sinclair Lewis, Georges Bernanos, Graham Greene—are treated, along with some lesser-known examples.

525. Detweiler, Robert. *Breaking the Fall: Religious Readings of Contemporary Fiction*. Louisville: Westminster John Knox, 1996.
This work draws from contemporary literary theory to enhance the religious interpretation of literature. Themes of special theological interest—suffering, love, and worship—are examined, with particular attention given to the work of Walker Percy and John Updike. Includes a select bibliography.

526. Ficken, Carl. *God's Story and Modern Literature: Reading Fiction in Community*. Philadelphia: Fortress, 1985.
An introduction to a theological appreciation of contemporary literature is presented in the first part of this volume. This is followed by five studies of individual works by William Faulkner, Flannery O'Connor, Ernest Gaines, Alice Walker, and Reynolds Price. There are extensive endnotes.

527. Kazin, Alfred. *God and the American Writer*. New York: Knopf, 1997.
A collection of twelve essays on writers from Hawthorne through Faulkner, by the late distinguished literary critic. An introductory essay outlines the whole phenomenon of the individual and even national sense of a quest for God, and the enduring interest in tracing the hand of God in America's affairs.

528. Mahoney, John L., ed. *Seeing into the Life of Things: Essays on Literature and Religious Experience.* New York: Fordham University Press, 1998.
The eclecticism of topics and writers is both the strength and the weakness of this far-ranging anthology. The first section considers broad theoretical issues, and the second section considers specific aspects of the work of particular artists.

529. Munk, Linda. *The Trivial Sublime: Theology and American Poetics.* New York: St. Martin's, 1992.
The work begins with a 21-page sampler of quotations on the relationship of theology and literatures. The essays that follow consider Emerson, Melville, Whitman, Dickinson, Frost, Edwards, etc., from a theological perspective. There are extensive notes and indexes.

530. Phillips, D. Z. *From Fantasy to Faith.* New York: St. Martin's, 1991.
This is a fine introduction to the interrelationship between contemporary literature and theological concerns. The individual essays explore critical religious issues in the work of writers as diverse as L. Frank Baum, Barbara Pym, Flannery O'Connor, Ernest Hemingway, and Albert Camus. (Example: a chapter titled "Displaced Persons" on the novels of Edith Wharton.) Footnotes accompany each chapter, and brief indexes conclude the book.

531. Rosenthal, Peggy. *The Poets' Jesus: Representations at the End of the Millennium.* Oxford and New York: Oxford University Press, 2000.
This book spends one chapter surveying poetic treatments of Jesus in the first 18 centuries A.D., and the remaining eight chapters bringing the discussion up to date under a variety of themes and cultural considerations. Notes are extensive.

532. Salyer, Gregory, and Robert Detweiler, eds. *Literature and Theology at Century's End.* Atlanta: Scholars Press, 1995.
This volume has an introductory essay, seven essays (of a somewhat technical nature) on Theory and Theology, and eight more essays on Writers and Text, treating specific themes or questions in the work of modern authors, including Murdoch, Morrison, Atwood, and others. Each chapter has extensive notes. There is a general index.

533. Timmerman, John H., and Donald R. Hettinga. *In the World: Reading and Writing as a Christian.* Grand Rapids: Baker, 1987.
This work is set out as a general introduction to the phenomena of language, writing, and literature within a Christian theological context.

The authors map out the terrain with their own introductory material and discussion questions, and provide a rich selection of readings under various themes, such as religion, ethics, science, psychology, etc.

534. Wright, Terence R. *Theology and Literature*. Oxford and New York: Blackwell, 1988.

The author contends that "it is possible and even necessary to talk about God in the forms of stories, poems, and plays" (p. vii). His work brings together the respective tasks of the theologian and the literary critic within various literary forms, such as the book of Genesis, the Gospel According to Mark, and other more contemporary structures. Includes extensive notes, a select bibliography, and an index.

535. Zinsser, William, ed. *Going on Faith: Writing as a Spiritual Quest*. New York: Marlowe, 1999.

A good selection of reflections by six different authors (including Frederick Buechner and Jaroslav Pelikan) on their own lives and work, edited and introduced by a master teacher of writing. A bibliography and notes on contributors are included. (Updates Zinsser's earlier volume, *Spiritual Quests*.)

Glossary: Types and Functions of Reference Books[*]

The titles and terminology that describe types of reference books are not always used with precision. Here is an outline of what ought generally to be expected from a work of a certain designation, with examples of sources cited in the present work.

Anthology (or Reader)—a collection of excerpts from writings under a stated theme or subject. The best of these provide introductions to selections or chapters, bibliographies that direct the reader to complete works of those whose selections are included in the anthology, etc. Example: Mark Kiley, ed., *Prayer from Alexander to Constantine: A Critical Anthology* (London and New York: Routledge, 1997).

Atlas—a collection of maps together with notes and an index of place names. A historical atlas outlines changes in boundaries of peoples, nations, languages, or religious groups over broad periods of time.

---

[*]I am indebted both for the idea of including a glossary and for some of the definitions used here to William M. Johnston's *Recent Reference Books in Religion: A Guide for Students, Scholars, Researchers, Buyers & Readers*, rev. ed. (Chicago: Fitzroy-Dearborn, 1998). Its glossary is on pages 29–37.

Example: Bret E. Carroll, *The Routledge Historical Atlas of Religion in America* (New York and London: Routledge, 2000).

Bibliography—a list of writings relating to a given subject. An **Annotated Bibliography** includes brief notes summarizing the contents of the individual items listed.

Commentary—a collection of chapter-by-chapter or verse-by-verse explanations of either a portion or the whole of Scripture. Commentaries may be written by individual scholars, who are commonly assigned, based on their interests and expertise, to write on a particular book. There are usually introductory essays. Examples: James L. Mays, ed. *The HarperCollins Bible Commentary* (San Francisco: HarperSanFrancisco, 2000), and I. Howard Marshall, *A Critical and Exegetical Commentary on the Pastoral Epistles* (Edinburgh: T. & T. Clark, 1999).

Companion—an introduction to a field of research, usually arranged alphabetically, and designed for self-teaching. Differs from a dictionary mainly in treating a smaller selection of topics, but at greater length. Example: Alister E. McGrath, ed., *The Blackwell Encyclopedia of Modern Christian Thought* (Cambridge, Mass.: Blackwell, 1993).

Concordance—an alphabetical index of all the words in a text or corpus of texts, showing every contextual occurrence of a word.

Dictionary—an alphabetically arranged collection of articles on persons, places, practices, and events related to a given subject. Usually differs from an encyclopedia in being composed of shorter articles. Example: Craig E. Evans and Stanley A. Porter, eds., *Dictionary of New Testament Background* (Downers Grove, Ill.: InterVarsity Press, 2000).

Encyclopedia—the most comprehensive of reference works, usually aiming for something approaching an exhaustive treatment. Traditionally an encyclopedia has been a multivolume collection of commissioned articles, arranged alphabetically, to include bibliography, cross-references, etc. Example: Geoffrey Bromiley, ed. and trans., *The Encyclopedia of Christianity*, 5 vols. projected (Grand Rapids: Eerdmans; Leiden: Brill, 1999–).

Glossary—an alphabetical list of terms with definitions. Example: Dianne Bergant, *The Collegeville Concise Glossary of Biblical Terms* (Collegeville, Minn.: Liturgical Press, 1994).

Handbook—a compendium of articles arranged to describe and engage at length with the problems and history of a particular field of research. Example: John R. Hinnells, ed., *A New Handbook of Living Religions* (Cambridge, Mass.: Blackwell, 1997).

Introduction—a work in any genre that undertakes to introduce a subject to those not yet acquainted with it. The level of detail and complexity in such works may vary considerably. Example: Raymond E. Brown, *An Introduction to the New Testament* (New York: Doubleday, 1997).

Lexicon—similar to a dictionary, but essentially a more specialized kind of encyclopedia, in that it provides a greater level of detail than a dictionary. Example: Ernst Jenni and Claus Westermann, eds. *Theological Lexicon of the Old Testament*, trans. Mark E. Biddle (Peabody, Mass.: Hendrickson, 1997).

Sourcebook—a primary document, or collection of primary documents, of history, literature, or religion, on which secondary writings are based.

Who's Who—a collection of capsule biographies, arranged alphabetically. Example: Lavinia Cohn-Sherbok, *Who's Who in Christianity* (New York: Routledge, 1998).

Appendix 2

Other Works on Theological Bibliography and Research

Barber, Cyril J., and Robert M. Krauss. *An Introduction to Theological Research: A Guide for College and Seminary Students.* Lanham, Md.: University Press of America, 2000.

Bollier, John A. *The Literature of Theology: A Guide for Students and Pastors.* Philadelphia: Westminster, 1979.

Davis, John Jefferson. *Theology Primer: Resources for the Theological Student.* Grand Rapids: Baker, 1981.

Field, Clive D. *Theology and Church History: A Guide to Research Resources.* Manchester: John Rylands Library, University of Manchester, 1990.

Gorman, Gary E., and Lyn Gorman. *Theological and Religious Reference Materials.* Vol. 1: *General Resources and Biblical Studies.* Westport, Conn.: Greenwood, 1984.

———. *Theological and Religious Reference Materials.* Vol. 3: *Practical Theology.* Westport, Conn.: Greenwood, 1986.

Haddon, Jeffrey K., and Douglas E. Cowan. *Religion on the Internet: Research Prospects and Promises.* Amsterdam, London, and New York: Elsevier Science, 2000.

Harvey, John F. *Scholarly Religious Libraries in North America: A Statistical Examination.* Lanham, Md., and London: Scarecrow, 1999.

Johnston, William J. *Recent Reference Books in Religion: A Guide for Students, Scholars, Researchers, Buyers & Readers.* Rev. ed. Chicago: Fitzroy-Dearborn, 1998.

Kepple, Robert J., and John R. Muether. *Reference Works for Theological Research.* Lanham, Md.: University Press of America, 1991.

Krupp, Robert A. *A Primer on Theological Research Tools.* Lanham, Md.: University Press of America, 1990.

Mann, Thomas. *The Oxford Guide to Library Research*. New York and Oxford: Oxford University Press, 2000.

McIntosh, Lawrence. *Religion and Theology: A Guide to Current Reference Sources*. Wagga Wagga, NSW, Australia: Center for Information Studies, 1997.

Sayre, John L. *Tools for Theological Research*. Enid, Okla.: Seminary Press, 1991.

Sheehy, Eugene P., ed. *Guide to Reference Books*. Chicago: American Library Association, 1992.

Thorsen, Donald A. D. *Theological Resources for Ministry: A Bibliography of Works in Theological Studies*. Nappanee, Ind.: Evangel, 1996.

Trotti, John B. *Aids to a Pastor's Library*. Missoula, Mont.: Scholars Press for the American Theological Library Association, 1977.

Ward, Carol. *The Christian Sourcebook*. New York: Random House, 1986.

Wilson, H. S., ed. *A Bibliography of Basic Theological Books*. Bangalore: Program on Theological Education, World Council of Churches, 1990.

Appendix 3

The Literature of Theology
on the Web

In the preface I noted that contrary to common folklore almost all of the *newest* (and often best) resources for research in theology continue to be published exclusively in print form. Yet this should not obscure the fact that there are good, public-domain resources available electronically, and that they can be very useful. Here are some general observations:

- Web-based resources call for new kinds of discrimination— without a clear and tenacious idea of what exactly is being sought, for example, the Web is unrivalled as a time-waster— and one has to be prepared to adjust to inconsistencies in file format, interface, etc., to an extent never required by print resources.
- If print publications are not evenly distributed over fields of study, the imbalances are even more problematic with Web resources.
- Especially if a scholar has a preference for "classic" resources, which have proven their worth over time, and is prepared to accommodate lack of control over access (network and server disruptions), it is well worth having a range of topical resources in place, either as "bookmarks," "desktop short- cuts," or on a personal Web page.

- It is still unclear what role the Internet will fill in the scholarly process. Explanations vary (lack of consensus on file format, copyright issues, financing), but up to the present large-scale text-digitization projects in theology have not come to fruition. Adoption of electronic formats for scholarly journals in religion is still in process. This underscores that it is still an open question whether the Internet will prove to be most successful as a publishing medium (gradually supplanting print formats) or as a medium for scholarly exchange (e-mail, listservs, Web conferences), or possibly as some combination of both.

The following is a concise sampling of links to public-domain Web resources:[*]

1. **Basic Resources:**
   a. Major Sites for Research in Religion and Theology
   Wabash Center Internet Guide
     http://www.wabashcenter.wabash.edu/Internet/front.htm

   Religious Studies Web Guide
     http://www.ucalgary.ca/~lipton/

   Research Guide for Christianity (Yale Divinity School Library)
     http://www.library.yale.edu/div/xtiangde.htm

   b. Online Texts

   Online Books Page—Religion (University of Pennsylvania)
     http://onlinebooks.library.upenn.edu/webbin/book/
     subjectstart?BL-BX

   Christian Classics Ethereal Library
     http://www.ccel.org/

---

[*] The relative scarcity of links in some areas—practical theology, denominations, etc.—mirrors the shortage and weakness of available resources on the Web.

2. **About the Bible**
   Bible Gateway
   http://www.biblegateway.com/cgi-bin/bible

   Bible Study Tools—Crosswalk.com
   http://bible.crosswalk.com/

   Easton's Bible Dictionary
   http://www.ccel.org/e/easton/ebd/ebd.html

   NT Gateway—Bible Translations and Editions
   http://www.ntgateway.com/bible.htm

   Resource Page for Biblical Studies
   http://www.torreys.org/bible/

   The New Schaff-Herzog Encyclopedia of Religious
   Knowledge
   http://www.ccel.org/s/schaff/encyc/

3. **Bible Commentaries**
   Adam Clarke—Commentary on the Bible
   http://www.godrules.net/library/clarke/clarkerut1.htm

   Calvin's Commentaries
   http://www.ccel.org/c/calvin/comment3/comm_index.htm

   Jamieson, Fausset, and Brown: Commentary Critical
   and Explanatory on the Whole Bible
   http://bible.crosswalk.com/Commentaries/
   JamiesonFaussetBrown/

   John Gill's Exposition of the Bible
   http://bible.crosswalk.com/Commentaries/
   GillsExpositionoftheBible/

   Matthew Henry Complete Commentary on the Whole Bible
   http://bible.crosswalk.com/Commentaries/
   MatthewHenryComplete/

4. **The Church in History**
    a. **General Sources**
    The Catholic Encyclopedia
      http://www.newadvent.org/cathen/

    b. **Early Church**
    Ecole Initiative—Early Church
      http://cedar.evansville.edu/~ecoleweb/

    Ancient History Sourcebook—Christian Origins
      http://www.fordham.edu/halsall/ancient/asbook11.html

    c. **Medieval Church**
    Digital Scriptorium
      http://sunsite.lib.berkeley.edu/Scriptorium/index.html

    Internet Medieval Sourcebook
      http://www.fordham.edu/halsall/sbook.html

    Online Reference Book for Medieval Studies
      http://orb.rhodes.edu/

    The Labyrinth: Resources for Medieval Studies
      http://labyrinth.georgetown.edu/

    d. **The Reformation**
    Anabaptists
      http://www.anabaptists.org/

    Bibliography: General Works on the Reformation
      http://camellia.shc.edu/theology/Reformation.htm

    Center for Reformation and Renaissance Studies
      http://crrs.utoronto.ca/

    H. Henry Meeter Center for Calvin Studies
      http://www.calvin.edu/meeter/

    Project Wittenberg
      http://www.iclnet.org/pub/resources/text/wittenberg/
      wittenberg-home.html

The Reformation: Google Directory
http://directory.google.com/Top/Society/
Religion_and_Spirituality/Christianity/Church_History/
The_Reformation/

Texts Relating to the Reformation
http://www.mun.ca/rels/reform/index.html

e. The Church in the Modern Era
A History of the Christian Church (vol. 7)—Phillip Schaff
http://www.bible.org/docs/history/schaff/vol7/httoc.htm

History of the Modern Church (Catholic)
http://www.silk.net/RelEd/modern.htm

Internet Modern History Sourcebook
http://www.fordham.edu/halsall/mod/modsbook4.html

5. **Theology and Christian Thought**
The Catholic Encyclopedia
http://www.newadvent.org/cathen/

The Early Church Fathers
http://www.ccel.org/fathers2/

The Early Christian Fathers
http://www.ccel.org/r/richardson/fathers/htm/i.htm

The Fathers of the Church
http://www.newadvent.org/fathers/

Aquinas's *Summa Theologica*
http://www.newadvent.org/summa/

Calvin's *Institutes of the Christian Religion* (Beveridge translation)
http://www.bible.org/docs/history/calvin/institut/httoc.htm

Finney's Systematic Theology
http://www.ccel.org/f/finney/theology/

6. **World Christianity, Ecumenism, World Religions**
    Adherents.com
    http://www.adherents.com/

    Comparative Religions
    http://www.comparativereligion.com/

    Concise Dictionary of Religions—Irving Hexham
    http://www.ucalgary.ca/~nurelweb/books/concise/index.html

    Religion Online
    http://www.religion-online.org/

    Sedos
    http://www.sedos.org/

    Sources for Mission and Non-Western Christianity
    (Yale Divinity Library)
    http://www.library.yale.edu/div/missions.htm

    World Evangelical Alliance: Missions Commission
    http://www.globalmission.org/

7. **Christian Denominations**
    Catholic.Net
    http://www.catholic.net/

    Vatican
    http://www.vatican.va/

    Church of England
    http://www.cofe.anglican.org

    Anglican Communion
    http://www.cofe.anglican.org

    Greek Orthodox Diocese of America
    http://www.goarch.org/

    United Methodist Church
    http://www.umc.org/index.asp

Assemblies of God
http://www.ag.org/top/

Mennonites
http://www.mennonite.net/

United Church of Christ
http://www.ucc.org/

Presbyterian Church in the U.S.A.
http://www.pcusa.org/

8. **Practical Theology**
Association of Professors and Researchers in Religious Education
http://www.mtso.edu/aprre/

Christian Educators Association
http://www.ceai.org/

Internet Theology Resources: Religious Education
and Pastoral Ministry
http://www.csbsju.edu/library/internet/theorled.html

Theology Library: Education
http://www.shc.edu/theolibrary/edu.htm

Alban Institute
http://www.alban.org/

American Association of Pastoral Counsellors
http://www.aapc.org/

Academy of Homiletics
http://www.wlu.ca/~wwwsem/ah/ahindex.shtml

College of Preachers
http://www.collegeofpreachers.org/

9. **Christian Spirituality**
Celtic Christian Spirituality
http://www.orthodoxinfo.com/general/celtic.htm

Center for Christian Spirituality
http://www.thecentre.com.au/

Christian Mysticism
http://www.innerexplorations.com/chmystext/christia.htm

Spiritual Writings (Anthology)
http://homechurch.org/spirituality/

10. **Christianity and Literature**
A Guide to Christian Literature on the Internet
http://www.iclnet.org/pub/resources/christian-books.html

Guide to Literary Study: Christianity and Literature (Wheaton College)
http://www.wheaton.edu/english/resources/litguide/christianity.html

ArtsReformation.com
http://www.artsreformation.com/

English Literature and Religion
http://www.inform.umd.edu/ENGL/englfac/WPeterson/ELR/elr.htm

Index of Authors and Editors

(Names are keyed to the entry, rather than the page number)

Index of Titles

(Titles are keyed to the entry, rather than the page number)